THE
USAGE
ECONOMY

LOGiSENSE

Contact information for LogiSense Corporation at www.logisense.com

ISBN: 9781738260737 (paperback)
ISBN: 9781738260720 (ebook)
ISBN: 9781738260706 (hardcover)
ISBN: 9781738260713 (audiobook)

Ordering Information:
Special discounts are available on quantity purchases by corporations, associations, and others. For details, visit www.logisense.com

THE
USAGE
ECONOMY

STRATEGIES FOR GROWTH, SMART PRICING,
AND EFFECTIVE TECHNOLOGY MANAGEMENT

ADAM HOWATSON

This book is dedicated to the staff, partners and customers of LogiSense Corporation and is made possible by their collective knowledge, innovation, and vision.

A special thanks the book's contributors, and in particular, Tim Neil and Dan Good, without whom the book would have remained a collection of thoughts.

TABLE OF CONTENTS

SECTION I

THE USAGE ECONOMY

SECTION II

THE FUTURE IS HERE

SECTION III

IMPLEMENTATION AND RESULTS

00/ INTRODUCTION

THE USAGE ECONOMY HAS ARRIVED—AND COMPANIES THAT AR- en't driving or adapting to the changing business landscape are going to be left in the dust.

Usage-based transactions (or usage-based billing), as the name suggests, are centred around **usage**. Customers pay for what they use— nothing more, nothing less. If you subscribe to a cell phone plan or wear a smartwatch, consume Amazon Web Services, use an avalanche beacon from Garmin, or pay a utility bill, you're familiar with usage-based economics.

Usage-based models are preferable for connected devices that gather and transmit data because they offer deep insights on consumer habits. Such models have primarily been used in IoT (Internet of Things), communications, and XaaS (Anything as a Service) technologies, but a multitude of other industries such as transportation and logistics, media and entertainment, and consumer electronics are also starting to explore and implement these models. Heavy equipment manufacturers are already making the shift to usage-based models. Cable companies are dying because they didn't.

The move to usage-based monetization is intensifying, not only because of consumer demand for these models but because of the finite nature of resources and the need for a more efficient world. Embracing the Usage Economy can help business owners to monetize every aspect of their companies, turn fair-weather clients into lifelong loyalists, and perpetually stay ahead of competitors.

The Usage Economy also offers business owners deep insights into their customers' wants, needs, and habits. Without understanding these usage patterns, your product pricing and service offerings all amount to guesswork. And guesswork isn't a great way to run a company.

From Ownership to Access

Business leaders may be focused on grabbing every last dollar they can from their customers, but in the Usage Economy, that kind of thinking can get a company in trouble. It will be the intelligence of the Usage Economy, not the brute force tactics of days gone by, that drives growth, expansion, and retention.

Think about the time before Uber. Before Airbnb. Before Netflix. These disruptors came in and ate one industry after another. Uber is one of the world's largest transportation logistics providers, and it doesn't own a car. The world's largest hospitality provider, Airbnb, doesn't own a brick. It was the unique commercial models and innovative software services of these companies that made them so prolific.

We've seen a pivot from ownership to access, and that pivot is for the better, though the very notion of that transition inspires visceral and polar reactions in different people. Regardless of your position on ownership vs. access, though, the old-timey notion of selling unused assets and being wasteful is so yesterday.

This is a change in the way we think about trade and our relationship with products and consumerism.

Consider our collective supply chains, which have been devastated over the past few years. At the start of the COVID-19 pandemic in 2020, a lot of supply was pulled forward, and we've since seen declining demand in a number of industries. The Organisation for Economic Co-operation and Development, or OECD, projected 3% global GDP growth in 2023, slowing to 2.7% in 2024.[1] That variability after a long period of sustained growth isn't easy on a supply chain. Add to that the occasional ship stuck in a canal, wildfire, flood, and bank collapse, as well as a sprinkling of other once-in-a-lifetime events, and you can see the risk and uncertainty in our world. Without trade and supply chains, life as we know it—certainly here in North America—ceases to exist.

Problems and uncertainties seem to be escalating.

As a result of this variability, transportation and logistics providers are accordingly evolving their commercialization models from a flat-fee tonnage-and-distance model to one involving variable costs for electricity and fuel and for features like refrigeration, storage location, special handling, and other factors.

You're not able to do that unless you utilize the tools that can track and calculate those charges.

1   "OECD Economic Outlook, Interim Report September 2023: Confronting Inflation and Low Growth," OECD, September 19, 2023, https://www.oecd.org/economic-outlook/september-2023/.

The X Factor

A company's value exchange represents the thing—the product or service—that customers are purchasing.

The value exchange for Uber is clear-cut. The customer orders a ride, the ride shows up, it takes the customer from point A to point B, and money for the ride is pulled from their account.

Lots of business leaders struggle to recognize their company's value exchange. They don't quite understand what it is they're selling that represents value to their customer. They get stuck thinking about appending a margin to their known costs, which is an approach that is out of touch with the customer's perception of the product or service.

Value can mean different things to different companies and their viability. It might not reflect margin on costs but rather the outcome of the product delivered. With usage-based pricing, the value derived by the customer can be priced discretely. This could be the number of times a service is used by a customer, a volume metric, or a specific outcome or event. The options are limitless, but companies must understand this value metric and have the technical capability to calculate and charge for it to implement an effective usage-based go-to-market.

In the IoT world, for example, a company could have sensors covering miles and miles of an oil pipeline. The sensors track oil flow, and they typically gather and send standard messages. But when a sensor detects a problem, the impacts could be catastrophic—and receiving that data could avert substantial financial and reputational risk.

Not all data is created equal. Providing sensor notifications when a boiler is overheating is more valuable, and should be charged at a higher rate, than providing an "all is good" notification. Or IoT devices that track trailers in different trailer yards can allow the company to charge differently based on location, where more expensive yards in urban locations are billed at a special rate compared to locations where space is not at the same premium.

There could be different rates based off the value of the data and the payload that's coming across the network. Or a company could be charged per incident or event where the customer sees particular value or where the "moment of impact" occurs with the customer.

This process is really about an introspection into your business— understanding your costs and values so that you can derive the most competitive and effective pricing for your customers. If customers clearly understand the value they're getting for their dollar, they'll stick around, be loyal, and provide a greater lifetime value to your business.

Digging Deep on Data

We have so much data available today that we didn't have previously, and it's at our fingertips. A company can know every interaction that every customer has had with every product and service, at what time it happened, what the duration was, where it occurred, etc. The company could then apply artificial intelligence or machine learning to that data to predict future customer trends. The telemetry generated through customer interactions and use of products and services is the source of a new gold rush. The emergence of large language model AIs into the mainstream through tools like ChatGPT is throwing fuel on this fire—but to have an AI that knows about your business, you need to tune it with your usage data.

Being able to interpret and analyze that data or feed it to an AI or machine learning engine can drive a company's innovation and ensure product and commercial decisions are rooted in the reality of how customers are actually consuming those offerings. If a company recognizes that every customer who buys product A comes back three months later to buy product B and service C, they can create a bundle of ABC, drive upsells, and get products B and C into the customer's hands earlier.

But these opportunities will never reveal themselves until you understand what is actually happening mechanically within the business at a granular level.

In one company we worked with, the gap between customer usage and billing was significant. Turns out, the company should have been billing customers 300% more than they had been.

The company had to call a board meeting to discuss how they would approach this situation—the magnitude of delta was that significant. Before implementing a usage-based system, the business was letting two-thirds of its revenue walk out the door, and they had no idea because they couldn't count it and couldn't monetize it.

Ostriches and Hawks

Change can be scary, especially if you've been doing something a certain way forever. But change is constant. Change is relentless. Change is undefeated.

When confronted with change, companies often take the approach of either the ostrich or the hawk. The ostrich buries its head in the sand. The hawk, on the other hand, circles overhead and scans for prey and opportunities.

Avoiding challenges and playing it safe in the Usage Economy—operating like the ostrich—can cause your company to go the way of the dodo. Or the dinosaurs. Or Blockbuster.

On the other hand, companies that take the lead in their industry effectively reset the chess board in their own favour. Their products and services are more transparent to customers and easier to use and upsell. Current customers are less apt to walk away because they don't feel ripped off, and customers currently with the competition transfer their service, loyalty be damned, because it's fairer. This is true in both B2B and B2C scenarios.

About Me—And My Goal

My insights on usage-based billing have been shaped by my tenure as CEO of LogiSense, a global leader in usage-based and subscription billing solutions. As our saying goes, "Billing shouldn't be painful."

LogiSense started in 1995 as an internet service provider. This was in the days before you would get internet service from a tier-one telecom provider, back when the internet was made up of T1 lines and racks of dial-up modems you would call in through your telephone line. You would call in through your telephone line to download a one-megabyte file that would take you 24 hours, then somebody would inevitably pick up the phone halfway through, and you'd have to start all over again.

In the company's early years, LogiSense established software around usage-based billing and counting how many minutes people were connected and how many kilobytes were downloaded, and that was a differentiator. The billing software, not the ISP operation, was the company's destiny.

So we shifted our focus to back-end billing tools. We sold our sophisticated usage-based billing software to all sorts of companies—consumer electronics providers, travel companies, IoT companies, and organizations around the world. Over the decades, we've become a usage-based billing platform provider.

I wrote this book with the goal of sharing insights on the Usage Economy to better prepare today's and tomorrow's business leaders. In the chapters ahead, you'll learn all about the advantages and opportunities with usage-based billing, as well as strategies for successful implementation, which will help you stand apart and stay relevant in a crowded and competitive global marketplace.

THE USAGE ECONOMY

Let's take a deeper look at the Usage Economy, study different transaction models, and highlight some key disruptions and trends that are transforming our world.

01 / THE USAGE ECONOMY EXPLAINED

ENVISION A PARKING LOT AT AN OFFICE PARK WITH 100 cars. That's 100,000 pounds of metal, which consumed who knows how many tons of carbon to produce, sitting idle. Those assets are not being utilized at 100% of their efficiency.

Do you want to buy tons of metal that sit unused in the driveway 23 hours a day, rusting away? Or do you want to have a car available only when you need it?

There must be a better way.

Ten cars could probably service that building of 100 people if they were utilized to 100%. Each person could pay to use a car for an hour to get them to and from where they were going instead of each person having their own car.

This is what I mean when I say that the Usage Economy is economics at the atomic level.

Instead of thinking of the traditional transaction model—where a customer buys an item like a pen or car or box of cereal, and ownership transfers from seller to buyer—zoom in to view products and services at their most basic form, such as these:

→ Data used

→ Kilometres travelled

→ Electricity consumed

→ Fuel burned

→ Square metres used

→ Duration of service sustained

→ API calls made

→ Serviceable hours billed

→ Carbon generated

→ Time connected

→ Feature entitlements included

→ Tonnage shipped

→ Digital assets downloaded

→ Hours viewed

→ Devices connected

If you can count a metric or measurement of usage, you can monetize it in a usage-based model.

Historically, we haven't been able to look at economic motion at this level of granularity. Now, because of technology and the usage telemetry it produces, we can—in numerous industries and infinite use cases. And this granular view is changing everything.

Atomic-level insights are helping businesses design better products and services while also causing customers to expect more of the companies with which they do business.

Cutting the Cord

An example we'll discuss often in this book is cable TV subscribers "cutting the cord" on their cable service and instead subscribing to streaming providers. With cable TV and its opaque, old-timey ownership model, you pay $4,000 a year for 500 channels whether you want them or not, and whether you watch them 24/7/365 or not at all, your rate doesn't change. You also pay to have advertising you don't want pumped into your living room.

On top of that, you need to call your provider every 12 months and sit on hold for hours before explaining why the company shouldn't hike your price even higher. It's a terrible customer experience and a worse commercial model.

It's no surprise that the number of cable TV subscribers peaked in the early 2000s and has been in free fall ever since, especially in the wake of so many streaming services. Consumers are smart—they don't want to pay for things they don't use. Younger people are especially indifferent about having a wasteful and unfair cable subscription.

The closer that we can get to monetizing at that atomic level, the better the transparency, choice, and value for consumers—and the more opportunities for companies to attract and maintain a healthy customer base.

Transparency

Customers have a clear understanding of what they're paying for with usage-based transactions. There aren't any surprises.[2]

No hidden fees. No unnecessary add-ons.

That transparency comes through in billing clarity. Bills feature detailed breakdowns of usage, cost, and impact. All the information and data points around usage can also help customers and vendors anticipate costs and performance.

---

2 Kshitij Grover, "The Three Benefits of Transparent Billing Practices," Orb, August 17, 2022, https://www.withorb.com/blog/billing-transparency.

A simple example of transparency in usage-based transactions involves cell phone plans.[3] Bills are broken down by voice minutes consumed, text or MMS messages sent and received, and data used each day and their totals. The user is alerted if they are approaching or pass data limits and is warned that their next bill may be higher than normal.

Choice

Usage-based transactions offer buyers flexibility, cost efficiency, and improved access to services. Customers can use as much or as little of a service as they wish and are charged according to their usage. This reduces the barrier to entry for a customer and can likewise reduce sales cycle length and help drive product adoption. Customers can also customize their service to focus only on things they need rather than paying for services they don't use, helping with retention and satisfaction.

If the customer is satisfied with their plan and service, they will continue paying for it. And if they aren't, they can change their plan or find another provider.

Flexibility is baked into the system—which is both an obstacle and an opportunity for companies.

Value

With so much transparency and flexibility, the value generated from products and services at that atomic level is very straightforward

---

3   "Understanding Your Telephone Bill," FCC Consumer Guide, last modified August 15, 2019, https://www.fcc.gov/sites/default/files/understanding_your_telephone_bill.pdf.

and clear. You pay for what you use, can change services as your needs change over time, and are presented with the evidence of your use/value at the time of commercial exchange. Clear as a bell!

Even if you aren't getting the most from your service or your needs do change—maybe you need an upgrade or downgrade in order to get better value out of your subscription—those changes should be easy, not punitive. Far too often, long-term deals can lock in customers with no visibility to what other options may be available to them, without any ability to change the plan if it no longer suits them. You may be able to get away with this for a while, but it ensures that when the customer does finally break through and takes action, it won't be to optimize. It'll be to churn.

There should be optionality with regard to the services you receive or the amount of data you can consume. Such flexibility can make you feel empowered instead of trapped, and it puts the power for upsell, expansion, and optimization in the hands of the customer. Of course, this assumes you have confidence in the value of your product.

A generation ago, everyone outside of the largest cities needed access to cars to get to and from work, which meant taking on car payments, and car insurance payments, and gas and maintenance costs, etc. Maybe they even needed to take on second jobs to pay for their cars.

These days, people who need to travel can do so with the tap of a phone app. A driver will pick them up from a specific location and take them to their destination, and the passenger will be charged for the single trip, and that's that. No car payments, no gas payments, no maintenance costs—just paying for a single ride. Better utilization of the asset, better economics for the customer and provider, and better for the world.

Experience

How do you get people to spend more money at a theme park without even thinking about it?

Disney removed the psychological and physical process of cash changing hands and replaced it with coloured watch-like bracelets called MagicBands that are linked to a prepaid deposit or credit card.[4] You wave your wrist in front of a sensor, and it's your fast-pass admission for rides, food at restaurants, souvenirs, tchotchkes, games … anything you want.

It's not money. It's magic.

Disney spent an estimated $1 billion on sensors, software, and infrastructure in rolling out the wristbands with the idea that the investment would drive greater upsell with park visitors.[5] After all, when you're at the park waving around your arm instead of reaching into a wallet, it's just funny money. This isn't real; let's just have fun.

It's pre-authorized; it's simple. You don't even have to reach for your wallet. There's no credit card, you don't enter a PIN—you just wave your wrist. It's a great example of monetization being part of the experience and the commercial design of a product influencing customer behaviour.

And think of all the usage telemetry—the gathering and automatic transmission of data through sensors and computing and network

---

4   "Disney Magic Bands Ultimate Guide," *The Frugal South*, last modified November 14, 2023, https://www.thefrugalsouth.com/disney-magicbands-101-plus-a-peek-at-the-new-magicband-2-0s/.

5   Brent Lorez, "Disney's $1 Billion Investment in the Internet of Things," LinkedIn, April 13, 2016, https://www.linkedin.com/pulse/disneys-1-billion-investment-internet-things-brent-lorenz.

power—Disney is gathering from park visitors while they're having their fun.

Refinement and Usage Telemetry

For pretty much all time, releasing a product or service amounted to guesswork. Companies have spent untold money on marketing and polls and focus groups, trying to understand what customers liked most about their product and how they engaged with it—all for outcomes that could be unclear, misleading, and biased.

With the emerging Usage Economy, however, there's much less guesswork.

That's due to usage telemetry. The Usage Economy requires the flow and exchange of information—which in turn can help service providers to design products and services better attuned to customers' needs. It can help to identify pain points, set competitive prices, and predict future usage patterns and revenue trends.

Refinement is a continuous process for any company—but with usage-based transactions, that process includes a fount of information instead of guesswork. And at the point of exchange, when a customer is paying a vendor, peace of mind comes in. There is comfort that customers are paying for a value they expect to receive.

Customers care about specific things. When most people buy a car, they're not focused on the particular alloy of sheet metal used for the body or the type of plastic coating the spark plug wires. They want to know how safe the car is, how fast it goes, how much it costs, and what its gas mileage is.

Through ongoing refinement, usage telemetry can help companies make better products until, in essence, they've developed the ideal product.

A Deepened Customer Experience

Garmin has developed a number of innovative connected devices and has deployed fishfinders, glass cockpits, avalanche beacons, and smartwatches around the world.

When the pandemic hit in 2020, national parks were closed, and people were stuck indoors due to lockdown orders. People had subscriptions to devices, and it wasn't clear when they would be able to use them again.

If you were paying for something you weren't using, your first thought would be "Let me cancel my subscription." To Garmin, that represented a real risk. Once a customer has terminated that commercial relationship, taken their credit card off file, and deactivated their device, there's now a much larger barrier to reactivating it.

When you have a customer base paying for a service they can't use during a pandemic, nothing good is going to happen—I can tell you that much. So Garmin took action to alleviate the customer concerns, knowing that a satisfied, robust, long-term subscription base was much more valuable than a quick score that would have left many customers feeling frustrated and ripped off.

Garmin worked with LogiSense to implement "state-based pricing" and offer a pandemic idle state to their customers. The company urged customers not to terminate their relationships, and they suspended charges for some devices until customers chose to reactivate them.

Would you accept this offer, no strings attached? There's not a lot of reasons to say no.

Garmin had massive retention as a result and earned lots of goodwill from their customers.

Information as the Product

Increasingly, information is the product. There's a really good book by author Jeremy Rifkin called *The Zero Marginal Cost Society* in which he details the driving down of marginal costs—and the impact on the economics of goods and services that can result.

For instance, if I were producing cars but had to stamp each one out of sheet metal individually, I would have substantial resource costs in replicating the initial design investment I made on that product. But when selling software, digital content, network access, outcomes, or services, the cost to replicate the original "product" is near zero. Not to say these products don't require substantial R&D, but the actual replication cost is marginal.

A book like this one could have zero, or near zero, marginal cost that can be monetized. Then the information itself—such as metadata about who's buying the book—can become a product itself. It's like an infinity mirror, requiring only the ingenuity to find the right market and model to sell the information being created.

That's not true in every industry, of course. But usage telemetry can be valuable in many ways. Let's say you run a mining company, for example, and you rent trucks to haul away mined materials from the mining site. The usage telemetry could involve how full the trucks are. If, all of a sudden, half of the dump trucks are being driven away empty, you've got real-time insight into your operation. The mining deposit might be running short. Or maybe there's a problem with your blasting crew. Or perhaps you have rented too many trucks.

The information gap between companies that embrace these practices by deploying the infrastructure necessary for a Usage Economy is akin to the gap between a Stone Age hunter-gatherer and a cell phone-using human being in 2023. One is walking around with the collective knowledge of humankind in their pocket on a black rectangle. The other is lugging a crude spear.

///

KEY CHAPTER TAKEAWAYS

→ Deeper usage telemetry is helping us to view products and services in their most basic, granular form.

→ Atomic-level insights are helping businesses design better products and services while also causing customers to expect more of the companies with which they do business.

→ Transparency and flexibility lead to customer value and a more fulfilling customer experience.

02/ DIFFERENT USAGE MODELS

I DON'T KNOW ABOUT YOU, BUT EVERY DAY I FEEL MORE AND more ripped off by the companies with which I interact as a consumer. It's the reason I no longer have a cable subscription.

Why should I pay hundreds of dollars every month for access to 500 channels I don't watch, just so I can have access to the handful of channels I do watch? Instead, I'd rather pay $20 a month for a streaming platform from a company with which I have a direct relationship.

This shift in billing really started with cell phone providers, but it's proliferated in recent years. Consumers are paying closer attention to the things they don't use or need.

Studies back up that sentiment. More than half of the participants in a 2022 Kearney Consumer Institute survey wanted to spend less than $50 a month on subscriptions. According to Kearney, "Forty percent of consumers think they have too many subscriptions—and we suspect that number will only increase."[6]

Think of all your subscriptions: Netflix, Hulu, Spotify, cell phone, internet, websites, gym membership, subscription boxes, pet food, news services, etc. What begins as one subscription can quickly become overwhelming, and sometimes companies even implement dark patterns on their digital properties to make it difficult for you to unsubscribe when you no longer desire access to their services.

Consumers want to pay a fair price for products and services—and they want to receive value that's commensurate to that cost. Usage-based billing is a great way to keep those two things in alignment, both in our consumer lives and in B2B environments.

But subscriptions are only one usage-based transaction model. Usage-based economics encompass a whole spectrum of transaction models. What's more, each model is associated with a different amount of risk for buyers and sellers.

In a completely non-usage-based model, the **traditional transaction**, a consumer buys a thing from the seller, they pay an amount of money for that thing on the spot, ownership of the thing is transferred, and the transaction is complete. There is no further obligation for either party.

There's also a **transaction plus maintenance or support model**, which is common in everything from heavy manufacturing to enterprise software. If you were to buy a swing shovel or a jet engine, you might have a recurring maintenance tail attached to that product or service to keep it viable and under warranty and eligible for upgrades.

---

6   Greg Portell and Katie Thomas, "The Subscription Apocalypse," Kearney, March 30, 2022, https://www.kearney.com/industry/consumer-retail/article/-/insights/the-subscription-apocalypse.

A **subscription-based model** involves a recurring charge for access to a product or service. Customers pay a period fee, typically monthly or annually. Common examples include Netflix for movies, Spotify for music, and gym memberships.

The next type of transaction involves a **commitment plus usage model**. Cell phones are a great example of this. When you buy a new phone, you can get locked into a contract to pay $100 a month for two years, and this arrangement will entitle you to a certain amount of usage. You will pay back the phone over time, and if you go over the set usage limits, you will incur additional charges.

In a **consumption drawdown** or **usage drawdown model**, the customer prepays an amount and draws down against it. Cloud providers like Amazon Web Services operate this way, offering variability for the consumer along with some certainty for the vendor. Prepaid toll payment devices work similarly—you put $50 or $100 on your account, and it automatically draws down whenever you go through a toll. When the money is depleted, it's up to you to add additional money to the account.

A **pure usage or consumption model** involves paying as you go— there is no capital expense and no forced commitment. Instead, the buyer is charged for specifically what they use.

The Right Model for Each Transaction

Some products and services, especially one-time assets, simply can't be sold through usage-based transactions. It wouldn't make sense, for example, for a buyer to rent an ice cream cone then give it back, melted and messy, after they didn't eat it. And homes couldn't be purchased this way either. I wouldn't want a usage-based agreement on owning my house. I might come back to find someone else had moved in because I suspended my usage while at work!

This isn't to say that usage-based transactions are doing away with other models—simply that they are becoming more prevalent.

Example: Wink

About 10 years ago, I went on a home-automation kick and replaced every light switch in the house with these fancy Lutron Caseta dimmers that you can connect with over radio frequency. I installed motorized blinds and Bose SoundLink speakers that could connect with a home-automation hub. I got all these neat, connected devices. And the hub that automated it all was called Wink, by a company called Quirky.

I bought the hub for $50. I think I got it on sale at Home Depot. They're way more expensive now. There was no charge to use the hub. Wink's business involved sunk costs—operating servers and a network, along with a mobile app that would allow you to connect over the internet. And they had no vector to monetize the hub after it was sold. It was a one-time retail purchase.

A few years later, lo and behold, I got an email that the company was filing for bankruptcy and that Wink was being sold. Wink has since bounced around from one owner to another, but it took until 2020—after Alexa and Siri and other connected devices grabbed hold of the marketplace—before Wink's home hubs were paired with a monthly subscription model.[7]

---

7   "Introducing Wink Subscription," *Wink Blog*, May 20, 2020, https://www.blog.wink.com/wink-blog/2020/5/6/introducing-wink-subscription.

Wink, in announcing the shift to a subscription package, admitted that its previous transaction model didn't work.

"Wink has relied solely on the one-time fee derived from hardware sales to cover ongoing cloud costs, development, and customer support. Providing users with local and remote access to their devices will always come at a cost for Wink, and over the years we have made great progress toward reducing these costs so that we can maintain that feature," the company wrote on its blog.[8]

Think of all the untold revenue that Wink sacrificed by failing to offer a subscription model!

Think of the sunk costs that the company couldn't recoup. In essence, the business model could only lead to failure—more customers mean higher overhead, and without any additional revenue from previous customers, Wink would have to keep selling more and more devices to finance its ballooning costs.

I still have my hub, but it's unconnected. When Wink switched to a subscription model, I lost the ability to use the smartphone app, which was fine with me—I already had all the hardware. So instead of clicking a button to turn the house on when I'm five minutes away from home, I walk in the door and press one switch, and it's the same experience for me.

Wink was an early mover in the market—it predated Ring cameras—and it was a real leader in the space, with a beautiful piece of hardware. But they lost out because they had the wrong commercial model and didn't have the right value metric.

They only saw the hub, and not the desire to have a connected home,

---

8   "Introducing Wink Subscription."

as the value metric. They could have charged any old price for the hub. Wink could have given away the hub for free and charged $30 a month from day one for the service, and they could have been making a mint.

They could have used the monthly subscription revenue to fund more R&D to create a better application.

And instead of charging new customers from the onset, they turned around and told long-term customers like me, "You've had the smartphone app for free for five years, but now you have to pay to keep it."

Humans don't respond well to having to pay for something they used to get for free.

Wink was late in realizing that the actual value they were selling to the customer wasn't a little $50 chunk of white plastic—it was the experience of being able to turn everything on and manage it remotely with one button.

Risk

Each of these models comes with some level of risk.

With a traditional transaction, the risk is on the buyer—the buyer is paying for the product or service up front, and whether they never use it or use it every day is completely up to them.

But along the spectrum of transactions leading to a usage model, the risk shifts from buyer to seller.

With a usage model, the capital was put into making the product or service possible, and nothing is being asked up front of the buyer.

If the consumer doesn't use the product, they aren't charged. This requires the consumer to use enough of the product or service to return the investment for the seller.

You might wonder, "If there's so much risk to usage-based transactions, why bother? Why not stick to more traditional sales models and let the customer assume the risk?"

The answer: Because customers today are pickier than ever before. Why shouldn't they be? Markets are more competitive. Consumers have more information at their disposal—and more options to choose from—than customers of any era in recorded history. Reviews from other customers are only a few clicks away, and window shopping can be done on a phone or computer.

It's easier today for customers to browse until they find the best option for them. Taking on more risk in the commercial model as a vendor means less risk for the customer, and that means more opportunities to attract new customers, upset the competition, and drive growth.

Business leaders' own consumer experiences and pain points are shaping real-world applications. People don't come into work in the morning and take out their home brain and put in their work brain—it's the same brain. And those consumer biases bleed from one area of their life to another. If someone feels ripped off by cable companies, for example, they might assume that any vendor who approaches them is trying to scam them. They're going to be acutely aware of wasteful expenses and scrutinize business spending with a greater degree of intensity.

Without adapting to today's customers and meeting their needs, you leave the door open for others in your space to take the lead.

Diminishing Risk

This isn't an all-or-nothing proposition, and companies that adopt a usage-based model can take steps to diminish risk associated with a customer-first usage-based monetization approach.

In order to do so, business leaders need to do four things:

→ Understand their company's business model.

→ Know how much capital was deployed to deliver the product or service.

→ Settle somewhere on the transaction spectrum that represents what's best for customers.

→ Ask themselves, "What are customers expecting? What is the competition doing? And what makes the most sense?"

For a company that requires a high degree of investment to get its product available to the customer, this could mean a minimum commitment plus usage model—that is, customers pay a flat monthly equipment fee and then an additional fee for their monthly consumption.

A prepaid drawdown structure off-loads risk to the customer while still offering the customer optionality of products and services.

Maybe a really long sales process with a one-time transaction is favourable. Or maybe the service is so high quality, the company will bring on customers by offering them no risk at all because they are so confident that customers will wind up paying for premium service.

Businesses have to determine which area of the spectrum is right for their product while also taking into account customer expectations.

Changing customer habits have remade and upended entire industries. And companies that embrace usage-based models can guide change instead of becoming hostage to it.

///

KEY CHAPTER TAKEAWAYS

→ Usage-based economics encompass a whole spectrum of transaction models.

→ Each model is associated with a different amount of risk for buyers and sellers.

→ Companies that adopt a usage-based model can take steps to diminish risk associated with a customer-first usage-based monetization approach.

03 / DISRUPTION AND TRENDS

DISRUPTION IS A CONSTANT IN BUSINESS AND LIFE. BUT IT often sneaks up on you.

An industry leader entrenches itself, and when a new model emerges, it's initially derided. *That's not the way it's done.* Amazon started as an online bookseller. Netflix began as a through-the-mail DVD service. People couldn't see what was to come.

A new model that is simpler and more flexible and more user-friendly. Over time, more and more people sign up. Adoption drives innovation, and the model is shifted.

It's happened with Software as a Service (SaaS), cloud computing, ride-hailing and car-sharing services, trip planning, rental units, cell phone and internet data plans, etc.—and maybe your industry is next.

BlackBerry

Companies are filled with so many smart, innovative people. But they can get too focused on what they do well and struggle to pivot.

For BlackBerry, if the product didn't have a keyboard, they weren't really interested in pursuing it. Research in Motion (the makers of BlackBerry) dominated the market for advanced phones in 2008 and 2009, even as Apple launched the iPhone and the first Android model was released.[9][10]

As it turned out, users really weren't so interested in keyboards when they could use touchscreens instead.

As a Waterlonian, I've heard anecdotes that BlackBerry conceived products but never launched them because they didn't fit the company's corporate vision. Internally, the company scoffed at competitors like the iPhone, with its weird touchscreen model and poor battery life. You had to charge your phone multiple times a day—iPhone users were dubbed wall huggers because they had to continually find outlets to charge their phones.

BlackBerry thought customers valued *not* having to charge their phones for days at a time. Everything was about efficiency—its users valued efficiency.

But in fact, its users valued the browsing and visual experience that came with using iPhone and Android phones. It turns out that was

---

9 Shobhit Seth, "BlackBerry: A Story of Constant Success & Failure," Investopedia, last modified March 17, 2023, https://www.investopedia.com/articles/investing/062315/blackberry-story-constant-success-failure.asp.

10 April Montgomery and Ken Mingis, "The Evolution of Apple's iPhone," Computerworld, November 13, 2023, https://www.computerworld.com/article/3692531/evolution-of-apple-iphone.html.

more valuable to them than battery life.

BlackBerry's network was the most efficient—but Apple and other phone makers partnered with wireless carriers like AT&T, which opened up data usage and a new vector for monetization.

The user experience of the iPhone was so special that people didn't care if they had to plug in their phones in the middle of the day—something we're very accustomed to today. There was a fashion that came with Apple devices, such as the iPod with white ear buds.

Apple products were cool. You wanted to be seen with them.

This loss of connection with one's customers reinforces the business staple NIHITO—Nothing Important Happens In The Office. You have to get out and know your customers and understand what matters to them.

The zeitgeist of each of those companies shaped or skewed their perspectives in designing the way that they brought their product to market. Microsoft saw the phone as an operating system sale. BlackBerry saw it as a keyboard sale. And Apple figured out that you were actually selling social status and data.

But none of that should be a surprise. Look at the lineage of each of those companies. Microsoft is an operating system company—Windows is how Microsoft really took off.

The keyboard was key to the engineering principles of BlackBerry.

Drink your own champagne long enough, and you'll get drunk on it.

Electric Vehicles (EVs)

Companies succeed or fail based on whether they plant their flag in a true differentiating feature. They come up with a core belief, and they won't challenge it or continue to innovate.

EVs and car manufacturing are great current examples.

Some car makers—instead of hedging their bets or being open-minded about EVs—buckled down and became entrenched in their position around combustion engines.

Toyota has been a long-time leader in the hybrid vehicle space with the Prius and other offerings, but their engineering focus wouldn't move away from internal combustion engines. They wouldn't commit to electrical vehicles, and as a result, they fell further and further behind for EVs.

The company was too stubborn.

Then, in mid-2023, Toyota announced they will be able to produce solid-state batteries—which will be able to go much further on one charge—by 2027. This was a massive breakthrough! It came after Toyota slow-played, pushed aside, and tried to stunt the emerging potential of EVs.[11]

But 2027 is still a few years away, during which time other companies like Tesla will still be eating up or maintaining market share. Tesla, like Apple, is innovation-focused and will keep finding better and more efficient ways to manufacture cars. Even though Tesla has only been in the market for a relatively short period of time, they've

---

11 Lawrence Ulrich, "Toyota Teases Solid-State Batteries in 2027," *IEEE Spectrum*, September 26, 2023, https://spectrum.ieee.org/toyota-solid-state-battery.

continued to innovate their manufacturing process so that the more vehicles they create, the more efficient their factories are, and the more they can lower costs—not through a scale of material focus but through streamlined manufacturing.[12]

Mainstay car companies like Ford and GM remain stuck in the way things were done in Dad's and Granddad's eras.

In contrast, the experience people are getting from Tesla is a software experience. The car is a device; it can get upgrades "over the air" in the form of software updates.

EVs aren't necessarily popular because they're better for the environment; it's because drivers don't want to have to get their cars serviced and get oil changes and all the frustrating things you typically have to do with a combustible engine car. And they're willing to charge for 20 minutes at the charging station instead of spending 5 minutes at the gas pump for all the other conveniences.

It's a completely different approach to owning and driving a car. The Tesla approach, of course, comes with its own wrinkles, such as secret modes and add-ons and software patches.[13] When a hurricane bore down on Florida in 2017, Tesla increased the range of drivers' vehicles—basically providing a free, automatic software upgrade.[14]

A lot of companies are still in an old-guard way of thinking that gets

---

12 Norihiko Shirouzu, "Tesla Reinvents Carmaking with Quiet Breakthroughs," Reuters, September 14, 2023, https://www.reuters.com/technology/gigacasting-20-tesla-reinvents-carmaking-with-quiet-breakthrough-2023-09-14/.
13 Umar Shakir, "Tesla Hacker Discovers Secret 'Elon Mode' for Hands-Free Full Self-Driving," The Verge, June 20, 2023, https://www.theverge.com/2023/6/20/23767041/tesla-hacker-elon-mode-hands-free-full-self-driving-autopilot.
14 Brad Jones, "Tesla Boosted the Range of Cars in Hurricane Irma's Path," Futurism, November 30, 2017, https://futurism.com/tesla-boosted-the-range-of-cars-in-hurricane-irmas-path.

them stuck on entrenched ideas of what people want. But consumer habits usually change when a better, easier thing comes along.

Sears

For decades, Sears was the United States' biggest retailer—it became a national force through its mail-order catalogue and built a network of 3,500 stores.[15] It was a retail mainstay. But after other companies like Walmart and Target ate away its market share, Sears failed to pivot. It was stuck in its ways.

Amazon and other online retailers offered convenient shopping from home that in many ways resembled Sears's mail-order days. It took too long for Sears to connect with online shoppers, and the ordering process on the company's website was clunky and inefficient. Buying vacuum cleaner bags on Sears.com was an exercise in futility. The interface was wonky, and items took days too long to arrive. All the joy that generations of shoppers had had when visiting Sears got washed away when there was a better option.

When a company becomes the market leader, it's easy for them to get complacent. Something was working to get them to the top. When you're the top gorilla, you're usually not as scrappy and innovative anymore.

Through corporate sales and bankruptcy filings and store closures, Sears has fallen by the wayside. And if it happened to Sears—which redefined shopping—it could happen to any company.

---

15 Erin McDowell and Avery Hartmans, "The Rise and Fall of Sears," Insider, updated December 19, 2022, https://www.businessinsider.com/rise-and-fall-of-sears-bankruptcy-store-closings.

"New Ways of Doing Business"

Usage-based transactions both disrupt existing models and create further disruption.

According to a report from Deloitte University Press about disruption and usage-based transactions,

The pricing component of aligning pricing with use removes barriers to use and expands the possible market. However, this pattern is disruptive because it also facilitates new ways of doing business. One of the interesting new ways of doing business is that as a company implements the technology to facilitate a model that aligns price with use, they also gain much greater visibility into how their customers use the product. This in turn can generate greater insight into how they can provide even more value to the customer. These insights can potentially be used to improve the offering across a broad customer base, affecting businesses across a range of industries.[16]

It's how Netflix upended streaming and how Lyft and Uber flipped ridesharing upside down.

Usage-based car insurance aims to disrupt the status quo too.[17] You can plug in a little black box that tracks acceleration and braking and G-forces, and the algorithm determines that you are a safe driver and calculates a charge that is fair. That kind of system is appealing—it's fair and transparent and affordable.

Younger people especially like usage-based car insurance systems be-

---

16 John Hagel et al., "Align Price with Use," Deloitte University Press, 2015, https://www2.deloitte.com/content/dam/insights/us/articles/disruptive-strategy-usage-based-pricing/DUP_3058_Align-price-with-use_v2.pdf.
17 Karl Eisenhower, "Usage-Based Insurance (UBI)," WalletHub, May 31, 2023, https://wallethub.com/edu/ci/usage-based-insurance/14118.

cause they typically have a higher-risk profile, and higher costs, for insurance. The usage telemetry data can effectively price an insurance plan that accounts for proper risk. Without the data, the insurance company charges younger drivers as though they are the riskiest drivers—but maybe they aren't.

Ownership to Access

The Usage Economy is expediting the shift from ownership to access.

Remember when you used to collect CDs and DVDs and video games? You had to own physical copies of items in order to consume them—and you bought special towers and binders to protect your discs, and if they got scratched, forget it. Nowadays, consuming your favourite media is as simple as clicking play on your phone or TV. You don't own that media; you don't store it in a dusty disc binder in the basement. You have access to it at the click of a button—the experience is so much simpler.

Needing a ride or a set of wheels to borrow has become a lot simpler too. A generation ago, everyone had to own their own car or bike, use it 5% of the time, and let it collect dust the rest of the day.

There's this constant move to get the most value for your money. Consumers will pay for the value, but they don't want wastage—that's why people are cutting the cord on their cable TV subscriptions or holding off on buying cars for themselves if they live in a city with good public transportation.

If people aren't using something, they don't want to pay for it. And they shouldn't have to.

The Usage Economy Isn't Always Disruptive

Aligning price and usage isn't always disruptive. Sometimes, it simply creates a new standard that all participants must follow.

That was the case with "Power by the Hour" engine maintenance in the jet engine market, which was first introduced by Rolls-Royce and was later adopted by other companies.[18]

As the Deloitte University Press report states, "Power by the Hour was not disruptive because most of the market leaders were able to adopt the model themselves. The concentrated customer pool and lack of an underserved market allowed incumbents time to adopt the new model."[19]

The Next Frontiers

Aggregation and intermediation, oddly enough, may represent the next frontier in the Usage Economy, especially where media and entertainment are concerned.

It's common for customers to subscribe to numerous streaming services at once, which can add up, and some providers have bundled different services together. But instead of requiring users to subscribe to Disney+ and Netflix and Hulu and Paramount Plus and Max and Amazon Prime, what if some aggregate provider came along and charged for access to 10 vendors instead of just one? And better yet, what if your prepaid "usage bucket" simply deducted an amount for whatever content you consumed, regardless of the publisher or ser-

---

18 "Rolls-Royce Celebrates 50th Anniversary of Power-by-the-Hour," Rolls-Royce, October 30, 2012, https://www.rolls-royce.com/media/press-releases-archive/yr-2012/121030-the-hour.aspx.
19 Hagel et al., "Align Price with Use."

vice from which it originated?

We're already starting to see some of this crossover aggregation between services. Disney, for example, planned to cross-publish Hulu content on Disney+ in late 2023, with CEO Bob Iger highlighting the importance of a "one-app experience."[20]

Eventually, we may see a centralized model where you pay pennies at a time for the articles you read or videos you watch, with the option of going to any provider you wish. As a consumer, you're going to be much faster to spend those pennies, versus signing up for another subscription that you probably won't use in a way you feel is valuable.

The first company to develop that all-encompassing centralized model is going to win the market, in my opinion.

Another area where streaming and cable providers fall short—and subsequently, another opportunity—comes with charging for what consumers actually watch instead of charging a flat subscription rate. With the Usage Economy, consumers pay only for the content they consume. Their eyeballs are open, and photons are hitting them, and they are enjoying the show in front of them. Under that model, if someone left Netflix playing all day, they'd wind up paying more, but if they only watched two episodes a week, they might only get charged $2 or $3 a month.

In being charged $3 a month for what they watched instead of a flat subscription fee, customers wouldn't have a reason to wonder if it's worth it for them to maintain their subscription. They'd continue as customers forever because it's advantageous, convenient, and

20 Todd Spangler, "Disney+ to Add Hulu Content in 'One-App Experience' Later in 2023, Prices for Disney+ to Increase," *Variety*, May 10, 2023, https://variety.com/2023/digital/news/disney-hulu-one-app-experience-later-in-2023-1235609003/.

fair to them.

Aggregation has upended services like hotel bookings, and other offerings ranging from news consumption to electric car charging aren't far behind. Companies that broker in information can make existing industries better by providing a better, easier customer experience. Airbnb, for example, isn't a hotel—it's a software and commercial layer applied to a million individual hotel operators. It provides a cohesive experience with access to a wider range of vendors than any individual human could have. It would be impossibly hard to start calling residents ahead of your trip to Hawaii. "Do you have an Airbnb available for the 14th to 18th of this month?" you ask.

"No," they say, so you call the next homeowner on your list, then the next, then the next …

AI and Machine Learning

AI (Artificial Intelligence) and machine learning represent another frontier for usage-based transactions—but they require patience and know-how.[21]

AI itself is only as good as the data with which you have trained it. You can't go to ChatGPT today and prompt it to give you the solution to maximizing your business value. That may occur in the coming years, as it gets more and more advanced. But if you haven't put the system in place to capture all your customers' interaction and usage telemetry, no AI can give you an answer to a question based on a dataset that does not exist. This is where software vendors will take the lead, by capturing that data and making it available to the teams

---

21 "What Is Machine Learning?", IBM, accessed November 1, 2023, https://www.ibm.com/topics/machine-learning.

responsible for training a business's AI. If I train—or tune, as it's known—an AI with the specific product, customer, commercial, and usage interactions of my company, it can craft recommendations, predictions, and responses that are directly relevant to and based on my specific business. Without this data, AI is relegated to tasks that can be completed using general public knowledge or the bounds of the dataset on which that specific AI was trained.

So you need to be able to gather data, then put it into an AI or machine learning system to process it. Without this training, an AI can't know how your business operates, its history, or the relevant trends and metrics upon which to base decisions or recommendations.

Once you've got the usage telemetry in place, from there, as you can imagine, the sky–or Skynet!—will be the limit.

With AI, we're not waiting for a toddler to get smarter day by day and year by year—it's going to get smarter real, real fast. Are you going to be able to then train it with the specifics of your business's telemetry to get meaningful outputs? Is your business even thinking about this today? Or does it seem like science fiction?

Over time, as a hypothetical, OpenAI could require you to buy credits that pay for the electricity, computing, storage, and other atomic elements needed to form the "thought" or "response" you have requested. Extremely complex calculations with large context datasets will cost more than simple natural language queries that can be answered by the public-data training set, like "Why is the sky blue?"

How to Monetize a Synthetic Thought

AI models are expensive to run—they rely on amounts of computing power reminiscent of crypto mining. They are going to require more complex monetization in the future.

We've seen earlier trends from ownership to access, and the recent shifts have moved from subscriptions to usage. AI will be no different; it will be almost reminiscent of renting time on a mainframe so many decades ago. A well-trained, evolved AI with current and deep training in a specific practice, industry, or use case may cost millions or tens of millions of dollars—or more—to develop. This is too expensive for most companies to justify, but getting access to that model or a multitude of specialized models on a usage basis and sharing the cost across many companies or customers makes more economic sense.

You're buying access to this "brain"; you don't own it. The company that trained it and the companies that provided the training data own it. You simply need access to the proverbial oracle's wisdom. The value comes from the answers it provides, and that's what you're being charged for, one answer at a time.

The Usage Economy allows us to recognize the relationships between cost, usage, computing power, and impact—and understanding how all those elements work together is just the latest development guiding consumers and providers of these complex and costly futuristic applications.

///

KEY CHAPTER TAKEAWAYS

→   The insights gleaned from usage telemetry can, in turn, drive additional innovation and optimization of product and market positioning.

→ The information *is* the product, and your capacity to generate, manage, and leverage usage telemetry will become increasingly important.

→ Aggregation intermediation and the drive for customer experience will influence usage-based commercial models.

→ AI is quickly emerging, and making it "smart" about your particular business is contingent on being able to tune it with your business's usage telemetry.

THE FUTURE IS HERE

Now that we've taken a deeper look at the Usage Economy, studied different transaction models, and highlighted some key disruptions and trends, let's consider the factors driving the global economy toward usage-based monetization.

There are a lot of things driving the adaption of usage-based economics—and those factors are only going to become more urgent in the coming years.

In the chapters ahead, let's dive into some of those drivers: the social, political, economic, environmental, and technological.

04/ SOCIAL

MILLENNIALS ARE APPROACHING THE WORLD DIFFERENTLY than preceding generations—because they have to.

Those born between 1980 and 2000 happen to be the largest U.S. generation today, even bigger than Baby Boomers. They've come of age just in time to face 30 years of wage stagnation along with record inflation.

Money doesn't go as far anymore.

In Canada, if you're a 24-year-old who'd like to get your first house and start your life … good luck! Average home prices in the country were above $800,000 in mid-2023.[22] The situation in the United States isn't much better.

In generations past, there was a social contract and an expectation that if you worked hard and set aside some money, you could have your house and your car and your white picket fence and 2.1 kids.

---

22 Pete Evans, "Average Canadian House Price Rose to $716,000 in April—Up by $100K since January," CBC News, May 15, 2023, https://www.cbc.ca/news/business/crea-housing-data-1.6843592.

But that social contract has been broken. Today, you can work 60 hours a week and still not be able to afford a roof over your head.

A Brookings study attributed changing consumer preferences to the "circumstances that young adults face, such as being more indebted, delaying starting a family, cars becoming more expensive, or having a lower income."[23]

People trudge through life with the expectation that they're going to be bled dry. Companies are taking every last dollar from their customers, and it's impossible to reach solid ground.[24] Wages that were suitable a few decades ago are now not cutting it.

Retirement ages are being rolled back. People are frustrated. How long until people say, "Enough is enough"?

Rehydrating the Social Contract

For younger people—the consumers of the future—who've endured these broken social contracts, there are greater expectations for companies they do business with and lots of ground to make up.

That means opportunities for companies attempting to rehydrate that social contract through trust, honesty, transparency, optionality, and value for money—that is, companies that embrace usage-based economic models.

As stated in a Goldman Sachs report on millennials, they "have been

---

23 Christopher Severen, "Why Are Young People Driving Less? Evidence Points to Economics, Not Preferences," Brookings, March 24, 2023, https://www.brookings.edu/articles/why-are-young-people-driving-less-evidence-points-to-economics-not-preferences/.
24 Drew DeSilver, "For Most U.S. Workers, Real Wages Have Barely Budged in Decades," Pew Research Center, August 7, 2018, https://www.pewresearch.org/short-reads/2018/08/07/for-most-us-workers-real-wages-have-barely-budged-for-decades/.

reluctant to buy items such as cars, music and luxury goods. Instead, they're turning to a new set of services that provide access to products without the burdens of ownership, giving rise to what's being called a 'sharing economy.'"[25]

We're seeing an increasing social pressure on companies to not do old-timey things like engaging in deceptive pricing practices, opaque plans, and contract lock-ins, because those things just aren't going to fly with smarter, better-educated, technologically advanced, tired-of-bullshit demographics.

You can feel and see this change happening. There's a different type of consumer expectation today.

The Impact of Social Media

Social media has expedited that shift.

If someone had a bad customer experience a generation ago, they could complain about it to their friends, maybe write a letter to the company, and … that was that.

Today, customers can hop on social media and put the company on blast, feedback that is available for anyone to see. Or they can post a scathing review on Glassdoor or Yelp. And those reviews and customer interactions are visible to everyone for years and years.

The shenanigans are being revealed as the economics become more and more atomic. Think of the Airbnb rented for $200 a night with a ridiculous cleaning fee tacked on or surge pricing on ridesharing in the wake of a tragedy.

---

25 "Millennials," Goldman Sachs, accessed December 7, 2023, https://www.goldmansachs.com/intelligence/archive/millennials/.

The "gotcha" game—raking in profits however a company can—doesn't resonate with savvy millennials or Gen Zers. If a company is scammy, or even gives off a vibe of being scammy, they will never use it again.

With Airbnb, the company put policies in place around cleaning-fee shenanigans, but those sorts of flare-ups don't engender customer support.

The Value of Trust

At a certain point, a straw will break the camel's back. We're just not sure which straw.

People, more and more, are voting with their dollars, especially if they don't have as many dollars to vote with. They're going to support companies that offer them value for money and can clearly explain what they're getting for that dollar.

As a result of all these trends, trust is so crucial for today's customers. If a customer doesn't trust a company, they won't do business with it. If a company does you wrong, just like the bully in the schoolyard that comes up and kicks your shin, you're not going to be hanging out with that bully anymore. And that's something that companies need to embrace, particularly as we see consumer shifts happening.

The Flawed Promise of Perpetual Growth

The promise of perpetual growth was always a fallacy.[26]

---

26 Christopher Ketcham, "The Fallacy of Endless Economy Growth," Millennium Alliance for Humanity and the Biosphere, Stanford University, May 25, 2020, https://mahb. stanford.edu/library-item/the-fallacy-of-endless-economic-growth/.

Netflix is cracking down on people sharing passwords because it's run out of new potential customers. Facebook has approximately three billion users to keep up with Aunt Millie's cat photos,[27] but there are only eight billion people on the planet, and only a certain portion of those eight billion are connected digitally. Those who either already have Facebook or are actively not using it, users and non-users alike, have become entrenched on their position to use or not use the platform.

Eventually, every company will hit an empirical maximum on the size of their market. The answer, then, becomes a matter of lifetime value and retention, LTV (lifetime value) expansion, and beating the competition, instead of driving potential customers away.

Deciding to turn your back on customers will have adverse consequences. If you're not behaving and interacting economically, with trust and a social contract, there's going to be a price to pay.

///

KEY CHAPTER TAKEAWAYS

→ Customers are frustrated about feeling like they've been taken advantage of—and companies can rehydrate broken social contracts through trust, honesty, transparency, optionality, and value for money.

→ People are voting with their dollars more and more, especially if they don't have as many dollars to vote with, meaning trust is crucial. This is true in both business and consumer relationships.

→ Every company has an empirical maximum on the size of their

---

27 Simon Kemp, "Facebook Users, Statistics, Data & Trends," DataReportal, last modified May 11, 2023, https://datareportal.com/essential-facebook-stats.

market, reinforcing the importance of lifetime value and retention, lifetime-value expansion, and beating the competition.

05/ POLITICAL

WE LIVE IN A TIME OF CLASHING VIEWPOINTS WHERE IN-creasing polarization means that no one can seem to agree on much of anything.

Those on opposite sides of the political aisle haven't been this far apart ideologically in decades.

Left versus right. Liberal versus conservative.

Where business is concerned, one side may believe that businesses should succeed at the cost of human beings—that there is no social contract and that every benefit should be for the capitalists. These folks put businesses first over people.

On the other side, we have an emerging demographic with a more technocentric worldview that is well versed in emerging social platforms and business models. This group believes that there could be a better future, but we need to take some action to reach that future. They're optimistic but clear-eyed about the difficult steps forward.

The Great Divide

With the former group, expect deregulation, less concern about social or environmental factors, and a doubling down on fading industries such as oil and gas.

If that latter cohort exerts its political presence, expect more regulation around how nasty a business can be in the market.

Political pressure is going to empower one of these models—and legislation and regulation will follow to make that the fabric of our society.

I've got my money on those pushing for change and progression. The Usage Economy, by nature, isn't about greed. It's about a fair trade for value and only using the resources you need. It's about the sharing economy and maximizing our asset-utilization efficiency as a civilization. It's about an evolution of capitalism to accommodate the technological advancement and ever-increasing access to information that comes with each new generation.

Regulation

"Regulation" is a term that makes business leaders shudder. It can also influence—and in many cases stifle—adoption for usage-based models. Some jurisdictions, for example, have laws on the books restricting the full implementation of usage-based auto insurance (privacy concerns and data usage are major reasons).

Regulation can also inhibit companies from gaining a foothold in different industries. With telecom, there's no end to the different providers in the U.S. marketplace—AT&T, T-Mobile, Verizon, and on and on. In Canada, however, the field is dominated by Rogers, Bell, and Telus. And not surprisingly, with fewer options, the cost for wireless in Canada is among the highest in the world.[28] Reduced competition drives costs up for the consumer.

An independent telecom research firm, Rewheel, blames the situation in Canada on non-competitive practices.

"The Canadian wireless market is not national in scope. It is a fragmented wireless market, a stack of provincial mobile network duopolies and monopolies stitched together by extensive and possibly coordinated roaming and network sharing agreements," Rewheel reported. The research firm also noted restrictive, anti-competitive measures by the Big Three market leaders and "excessive and hence ineffective" national guidelines.[29]

Data Sovereignty

Data sovereignty is another area of so much difference between countries and continents.

Where is the data coming in? Where's it being held? How's it being examined? How is it priced? Which country's citizens will be processing the data?

Major providers need to open data centres globally just to store data from a personal information and data sovereignty standpoint. And then services need to be priced accordingly.

---

28 "The State of 4G and 5G Pricing, 1H2022—Country Rankings," Rewheel, May 2022, https://research.rewheel.fi/downloads/The_state_of_4G_5G_pricing_17_release_1H2022_countries_PUBLIC_VERSION.pdf.
29 "Root Cause of Weak Competition in the Canadian Wireless Market," Rewheel/research, September 8, 2019, https://research.rewheel.fi/downloads/Root_cause_weak_competition_Canada_wireless_market_PUBLIC.pdf.

Consumer Protection

Many jurisdictions, such as New York City, have made it illegal for businesses to price gouge for goods or services that are essential to health and safety.

Legislators have also focused on price gouging at the gas pump.

In September 2023, Canadian lawmakers introduced legislation aimed at stabilizing prices for groceries and increasing enforcement for price-fixing and collaboration that decrease consumer choice if further instances of price gouging emerge.[30]

Across Borders

Electric charging is a reminder of the importance of foreign partnerships.

In the United States, there are a handful of players. Across Europe, there are dozens of providers, sometimes country by country. And you have to have an account with every provider you wish to use. It's like the old cell phone roaming networks.

The challenge comes in when you have to make a trip from Scotland to the bottom of France using multiple different charging networks. Over time, that industry could evolve to the point where you have a single account that you pay across the different providers—but such a system requires collaboration between different countries.

---

30 "Government Introduces Legislation to Build More Rental Homes and Stabilize Grocery Prices," Department of Finance Canada, September 21, 2023, https://www.canada.ca/en/department-finance/news/2023/09/government-introduces-legislation-to-build-more-rental-homes-and-stabilize-grocery-prices.html.

The Need to Adapt

A major effort in recent years—one that encapsulates the political throughline with the Usage Economy—is the move for companies to shift to carbon neutrality and reduce greenhouse gas emissions.

The effort has been closely aligned with environmental causes, and major companies like Microsoft[31] and Apple[32] have made net-zero and carbon neutral pledges.

But those shifts closely align with usage-based models. Companies should want to know their carbon footprints in order to better monetize their products and services, and, perhaps more importantly, to comply with forthcoming or already-present carbon-reporting legislation.

This isn't a request to appeal to the soft side of your heart and ask you to become an environmentalist on the spot—it's a request to adapt.

If you don't, you're bound to screw up your business.

By the time regulation comes in, and by the time the generations that have the spending and purchasing power emerge into their full demographic strength, if you've got this wrong, your company isn't going to exist.

//

KEY CHAPTER TAKEAWAYS

31 Brad Smith, "Microsoft Will Be Carbon Negative by 2030," Official Microsoft Blog, January 16, 2020, https://blogs.microsoft.com/blog/2020/01/16/microsoft-will-be-carbon-negative-by-2030/.
32 Arbaz Ahmad, "Apple Pledges to Go Carbon Neutral," Power BI Themes Gallery, October 15, 2023, https://community.fabric.microsoft.com/t5/Themes-Gallery/Apple-pledges-to-go-Carbon-Neutral/m-p/3477425.

→ Political pressure will bring about changes in legislation and regulation.

→ Companies face different opportunities and obstacles based on the country or region and the guidelines in place.

→ Companies should want to know their carbon footprint in order to better monetize their products and services and to comply with forthcoming or already-present carbon-reporting legislation.

06/ ECONOMIC

THE ECONOMICS ALWAYS WIN, AND PEOPLE ALWAYS LOSE.

A million people can protest, and it might not change a thing—but if there are economic incentives or competitive pressure, human society will follow the dollar, for better or worse. With more transparent economics, and the power of social media, people are tipping some power back to their favour.

That was the case with drug maker Eli Lilly and Company, which spent years overpricing the drug insulin. The patent for insulin was sold for $1 by Frederick Banting[33] so that people could have access to it. But there we were, 80 years later, and you could pay $1,000 a month, or you could die.

People complained, but nothing seemed to change—that is, until competitors like investor Mark Cuban's Cost Plus Drugs compa-

---

33 "100 Years of Insulin," Diabetes UK, accessed November 1, 2023, https://www.diabetes.org.uk/our-research/about-our-research/our-impact/discovery-of-insulin.

ny announced that they would sell insulin for about $35 a bottle,[34] which factored in storage and refrigeration and shipping costs. By simply pricing drugs at reasonable levels, the company undercut Eli Lilly and presented itself as the affordable alternative. The commercial model was the disruptor.

As other, less expensive, options emerged, Eli Lilly was pilloried by the public,[35] lost billions of dollars in market cap, and was subjected to lawsuits and regulation threats for its shameless overpricing of insulin.

And then the company turned around and announced it would reduce the price to $35.[36] But it came too little, too late for customers. Trust had been irreparably damaged.

Because Cuban's company avoided price gouging insulin by using a more transparent and reasonable pricing structure, he's seen as the good guy because his company took action first. Credit to Cuban and his philanthropy to set this up of his own volition. His company's efforts put tremendous pressure on name brand prescription drug makers to compete with what he had done. And he is simply offering a fair, transparent usage-based model. This is one example where social and political pressure are forcing change in businesses.

There's still lots of profit to be made. And I'm not suggesting that businesses act altruistically, because businesses typically don't exist to

34 Berkeley Lovelace Jr., et al., "Mark Cuban's Next Act on Drug Costs: Tackling Insulin," last modified December 20, 2020, https://news.yahoo.com/mark-cuban-next-act-drug-004220797.html.

35 Kevin Dunleavy, "After Price Cuts, Eli Lilly Inks $13.5M Settlement in Long-Running Insulin Lawsuit," Fierce Pharma, May 30, 2023, https://www.fiercepharma.com/pharma/eli-lilly-inks-settlement-long-running-insulin-pricing-lawsuit.

36 Dylan Scott, "The Campaign to Make Insulin Less Expensive Just Scored a Major Victory," Vox, March 1, 2023, https://www.vox.com/policy/2023/3/1/23620246/eli-lilly-insulin-price-cap-cost.

do things altruistically—we're all here to earn a living. But if you're still charging $1,000 for a $30 product, you're liable to face blowback for it eventually. Life is good in the ivory tower ... until it's not!

Making as much money as possible is great. But it can cost you massively in the long run if it's done in a way that does not relate value and good faith to the customer—especially as those customers, due to usage-based economics, better understand the value of goods and services and their capacity to "out" bad behaviour increases with new technologies.

Something's Gotta Give

When you've got 40% of people in the United States who can't afford basic needs like housing, food, shelter, or medical access, something is bound to give.[37]

The dollar doesn't go as far anymore, forcing people and businesses to put a lot more scrutiny on the specific value that they're getting for their money. Being able to conflate what the value your product delivers with what you bill the customer for is becoming increasingly important.

As customers, we've all asked ourselves, "What am I paying for here?"

The Millennial Factor

We're on the precipice of a major demographic shift. Boomers are shifting out of the workforce, and those spots are being filled by

---

37 Michael Karpman, Stephen Zuckerman, and Dulce Gonzalez, "The Well-Being and Basic Needs Survey," Urban Institute, August 28, 2018, https://www.urban.org/research/publication/well-being-and-basic-needs-survey.

new workers and younger managers who understand the competitive pressure around usage-based models and have grown up experiencing a sharing system.

They're approaching business differently. And they have a better understanding of the value of money because their money isn't going as far as their parents' money did.

Think about all the price gouging that happened during the start of the coronavirus pandemic and in the years that followed due to supply chain shortages, both real and perceived.[38] The cost of eggs was up 70% in 2023. An avian flu accounted for some of the increase, but much of it was due to greed.[39]

Companies that ingratiate themselves through brand loyalty, lifetime value, customer retention, and additional sales stand poised to thrive in the Usage Economy. But those that continue to operate in the greedy or opaque ways of yesteryear are going to extinguish themselves.

Money's No Longer Free

In 2023 and beyond, money is no longer free. We went through sort of a silly period of 0% or negative interest—*I will pay you to take my cash!* What a wild concept. Things were positioned that way for over a decade.

But now it's time to pay the piper. As I write this, we're entering a

---

38 Rik Chakraborti and Gavin Roberts, "How Price-Gouging Regulation Undermined COVID-19 Mitigation: County-Level Evidence of Unintended Consequences," *Public Choice* 196 (April 18, 2023): 51–83, https://doi.org/10.1007/s11127-023-01054-z.
39 Mike Winters and Tasia Jensen, "Egg Prices Increased 70% over the Last Year—Here's Why," CNBC, March 3, 2023, https://www.cnbc.com/2023/03/03/egg-prices-increased-70percent-over-the-last-yearheres-why-.html.

forced recession in order to recover some of this inflationary effect.

There are a lot of businesses that had a growth-at-all-costs mentali-ty—it didn't matter what your story was, or how your business was doing, or whether it was losing money, as long as it was growing. But the music has stopped now, and investors are valuing business funda-mentals like retention and growth and recurring revenue.

Businesses want to stretch $1 further, and every chief information officer is scanning a list of expenditures, saying, "I spend $10 mil-lion a year in recurring software subscriptions. I want every depart-ment head to get in line and tell me why I shouldn't cancel every one of these."

Businesses that invest now in future and emerging economic models are going to be much better positioned to succeed in the coming years.

A Shift from the Monolithic

The more technologies become accessible to individuals, the more the economics can be broken down at an atomic level.

Think about the debate around non-renewable energy sources like coal versus renewable energy sources such as solar and wind. Res-idents in many jurisdictions can generate revenue by selling extra power back to the grid—a reverse usage-based model.

It's not feasible for most people to own their own coal plants or steam-generating facilities. But with solar panels, each resident has the potential to, in essence, become their own power-generating sta-tion and sell surplus energy back to the grid.

The ability to break things down and distribute them drives our society's economic model away from the monolithic. Eventually, the individual economics may win out. What is emerging is a network of networks. 1,000 solar panels on 100 rooftops, all monetized individually by the watt, forming a grid based on usage and contribution.

Software

I consider software the last great artisanal trade.

It involves individual human beings (at least for the time being—AI is evolving in this space too) together contributing their individual talents to an end product. Once the intellectual property has been created, the cost to reproduce the piece of software or grant additional access to it is near zero. And increasingly, the information that is generated, along with its metadata, also becomes a product.

With these emerging models comes the opportunity to generate additional monetization. Some companies get that process right, while others get it wrong.

One such example is Mercedes, which in 2023 rolled out a fascinating offering for consumers: pay more money and your electric car will go faster.[40]

The vehicle upgrades were available for $60 or $90 per month, depending on the vehicle, through the car maker's "Acceleration Increase On-Demand" upgrade.

People weren't quite sure what to think about the option. The actual

---

40 "Mercedes-Benz USA Announces Performance Acceleration On-Demand Upgrade for EQE and EQS Customers," Mercedes-Benz, April 26, 2023, https://media.mbusa.com/releases/mercedes-benz-usa-announces-performance-acceleration-on-demand-upgrade-for-eqe-and-eqs-customers.

car is the same either way. They paid for the physical asset, and it's sitting in their garage.

From the manufacturer's perspective, they developed the intellectual property to drive that greater performance—human beings need to write software, there has to be testing, and they need to take the cars on the tracks and put capital into deploying a heavily regulated product.

It's cheaper for Mercedes to make a million of the exact same unit of car and change the entitlements via software. And it's up to consumers to decide whether they are interested in paying for an upgrade.

At the end of the day, both models of car would be more expensive if you had to have two manufacturing lines. So the seller can always make the car capable of doing more and then monetize the "more" as an upgrade, as they did with power windows a generation ago.

Power windows weren't always a standard option, but by charging a premium for them, developing the technology, and repeating that technological development and production, car makers developed them to the point where it became cheap enough that now everybody can offer them, much like the difference between the 1993 solar panel and the 2023 solar panels—very different price points (about 90% cheaper) despite being the same technology.

In this—and in most cases—early adopters wind up paying a premium to offset the cost of that additional development.

The nature of products is changing economically.

The Usage Economy Drives Capitalism

In the end, as I stated earlier, *the economics always win, and people always lose.* And in a lot of ways, the Usage Economy can be used to advance capitalism *and* the interests of people.

If a company can use fewer resources to draw the same amount of revenue, while simultaneously driving a positive outcome for the environment and higher margins, great!

Usage-based economics isn't about asking businesses to give anything up. It's about helping them get further ahead by evolving to a modern, usage-based commercial approach. It's about getting the maximum utilization and monetization per resource consumed and keeping customers happy. The playing field is different now. The focus isn't how cheaply and quickly something can be done, nor is it pulling as many resources from the earth as possible. It's about making the most out of assets in a way that appeals to consumers and helps the business thrive.

If a company is doing that—and killing two birds with one stone— they can spend less money, make more money, and develop their business model in a way that will allow the company to exist 100 years from now.

Many companies put the environment first. And that's great. Your company doesn't necessarily need to, and that's not what I'm advocating primarily. But if you can cut your emissions by 90% while increasing your profit margin—*saving the world while making money*—it's tough to say no to that.

It's economics. And it doesn't matter whether you're part of Greenpeace or a staunch capitalist; there's no argument. This is all about the base needs of economics, resource use, and success.

It's getting that extra dollar and saving money while simultaneously building deeper trust with your customers.

///

KEY CHAPTER TAKEAWAYS

→ Making as much money as possible is great. But it can cost you massively in the long run if done in a way that does not relate value and good faith to the customer.

→ Money doesn't go as far as it used to, causing customers to be more vigilant with their spending. Increasingly the monetization strategy is a part of the customer experience and a part of your product.

→ The Usage Economy can be used to advance our business ambitions, our customer experience, and our environmental approach.

07 / ENVIRONMENTAL

A WILDFIRE BURNED ACROSS QUEBEC, CANADA, IN 2023, AND the smoke turned the sky orange on the United States' East Coast more than 400 miles away.[41]

Temperatures are rising. Polar ice sheets are melting rapidly.[42]

In the coming decades, we could be facing mass migration as sea levels rise. Will Florida become the next Rotterdam, existing under sea level with a series of dikes and dams? Or will we surrender that land to nature?

Regardless of where you stand on environmental issues, they will be front and centre for future generations.

As the saying goes, "Future generations benefit when old men plant trees in whose shade they will never sit."

---

41 Kenneth Chang, "Why the Wildfire Smoke Makes the Sky Turn Wild Colors," *New York Times*, June 8, 2023, https://www.nytimes.com/2023/06/08/science/sky-color-wildfire-smoke-orange.html.
42 Daniel Glick, "The Big Thaw," National Geographic, accessed November 1, 2023, https://www.nationalgeographic.com/environment/article/big-thaw.

We don't have the option to sit here and just hope this will work itself out. And due to the Usage Economy, that shouldn't even be a consideration.

Resource Scarcity

Usage-based models are all about getting more with less.

If we do face mass migration in the coming years, we're liable to experience more people in less space with fewer resources, requiring us to make the most of the resources we have.

Resource scarcity covers both the land and the resources the land produces. We're not making more land. But we are making more people, who will need to consume more resources.

Righting the Ship

The way we think of global warming and climate change is crucial. With the Usage Economy, every penny and every gram of carbon counts.

Maybe you don't feel that problem acutely today—some don't. The overwhelming body of scientific evidence suggests that we are very close to too late in terms of righting the ship on climate change and global warming.[43]

New systems are required that will allow us to better leverage assets and cut down on wasteful practices.

A 2022 United Nations report on population growth and sustainable

---

43 "How Do We Know Climate Change Is Real?," NASA, accessed December 7, 2023, https://climate.nasa.gov/evidence/.

development noted the importance of "lessening the reliance on fossil fuels and other non-renewable, high-intensity resources; increasing the efficiency of resource use; reducing emissions and waste from extraction, production, consumption and disposal; extending product life cycles through intelligent product design and standardization to encourage reuse, recycling and re-manufacturing; and promoting a shift in consumption patterns towards goods and services with lower energy and material intensity."[44]

Maybe the Usage Economy won't save the world. But it sure will help. If we can use 100% of what we make, we ought to make less.

Sharing Is Caring

If we don't have an economic incentive to get a greater utilization out of the goods we produce and the services we provide, we will continue to do wasteful things.

That is the problem that car-sharing services such as Zipcar and Turo aim to address. If you live in a city like New York or San Francisco, buying a car that's just going to sit there and eat up lots of money for parking makes zero sense—especially if you can quickly get a car whenever you need without the burden of ownership.

The more people use public transportation or sharing services, the fewer cars there are on the road.

A 2023 McKinsey & Company report projected that shared mobility could generate up to $1 trillion in consumer spending annually by

---

44 "Global Population Growth and Sustainable Development," United Nations, 2021, https://www.un.org/development/desa/pd/sites/www.un.org.development.desa.pd/files/undesa_pd_2022_global_population_growth.pdf.

2030.[45] Projections included a scenario in which "private-car ownership declines, roads become much less congested, and far fewer parking lots are needed, freeing up areas for play and recreation. As a result, city dwellers enjoy much more green space, including parks, playgrounds, and public plazas."

Usage and sharing models can benefit the environment even when the product or service's main goals aren't environmentally focused. Saving and preserving resources just makes sense.

Supply Chains

Looking at things at the atomic level forces companies to consider supply chain costs and inefficiencies—from the cost of oil to refrigeration to storage.

With each element in the supply chain discretely monetizable, wasteful efforts and unnecessary costs are much easier to find and root out. Companies that previously left inventory in cold storage for six months will reconsider if they're charged by the kilowatt and cubic footage of refrigerated storage.

All of that telemetry can help companies to keep less inventory on hand.

And it can help us diminish supply chain shenanigans like sending peaches grown in Brazil or Chile to Taiwan to be packaged and shipped to North America to be grabbed off grocery store shelves.

If I were charged directly commensurate with the exact distance

---

45 "Shared Mobility: Sustainable Cities, Shared Destinies," McKinsey & Company, January 5, 2023, https://www.mckinsey.com/industries/automotive-and-assembly/our-insights/shared-mobility-sustainable-cities-shared-destinies.

travelled and the cost of refrigeration and safekeeping, I probably wouldn't ship peaches around the world twice—I would start buying Georgia peaches and can them in Atlanta, then sell them in Marietta.

Better Collective Outcomes

The environmental factor probably feels impossible or insurmountable right now—but when we put our heads together, we're capable of taking huge, collective actions. Sometimes we get it right through legislation and cooperation, like the efforts to improve the ozone layer. Scientists collectively determined the problem, a treaty was put in place, and we significantly reduced our usage of chlorofluorocarbons.

Here we are in 2023, and our ozone is on the mend.[46]

Human beings aren't intrinsically good with the abstract. But good common sense—creating economic systems at an atomic level—can help us to drive basic human behaviour toward a better collective outcome.

The Environmental-Tech Crossover

There's a strong crossover between technical and environmental factors.

Cryptocurrency assets take up *a lot* of electricity—somewhere in the vicinity of 120 to 240 billion kilowatt-hours per year. This exceeds

---

46 "Rebuilding the Ozone Layer: How the World Came Together for the Ultimate Repair Job," UN Environment Programme, September 15, 2021, https://www.unep.org/news-and-stories/story/rebuilding-ozone-layer-how-world-came-together-ultimate-repair-job.

the yearly electricity usage of countries like Australia.[47] That's a massive power drain to keep virtual dollars in existence. It's a similar situation with AI. The tech revolution is going to be very carbon intensive, driven by large data centres.

In recent years, Amazon Web Services has emitted more than 70 million metric tons of carbon dioxide equivalent.[48] Every Google search causes emissions.[49]

Another example of the environmental-tech crossover is the electrification of transportation, which involves rare earth minerals that are scarce. The whole world wants to change over to electric vehicles, but constructing an electric vehicle requires more carbon than constructing a gasoline car. (EVs, when driven, emit far less CO_2, so the environmental impact balances out over time.)[50]

Accounting for our carbon footprint isn't easy and can require us to consider elements like clothing, water usage, bottles, and streaming online videos.[51]

New technologies are great and exciting, but there's more than just regulatory, compliance, and ethical issues behind them—there's also

47 "Face Sheet: Climate and Energy Implications of Crypto-Assets in the United States," The White House, September 8, 2022, https://www.whitehouse.gov/ostp/news-updates/2022/09/08/fact-sheet-climate-and-energy-implications-of-crypto-assets-in-the-united-states/.

48 Matt Day, "Amazon Says Its Carbon Emissions Fell for First Time in 2022," *Spokesman-Review*, last modified July 18, 2023, https://www.spokesman.com/stories/2023/jul/18/amazon-says-its-carbon-emissions-fell-for-first-ti/.

49 Anne Quito, "Every Google Search Results in CO2 Emissions. This Real-Time Data Viz Shows How Much," Quartz, May 7, 2018, https://qz.com/1267709/every-google-search-results-in-co2-emissions-this-real-time-dataviz-shows-how-much.

50 Andrew Moseman and Sergey Paltsev, "Are Electric Vehicles Definitely Better for the Climate than Gas-Powered Cars?" MIT, October 13, 2022, https://climate.mit.edu/ask-mit/are-electric-vehicles-definitely-better-climate-gas-powered-cars.

51 "10 Surprising Sources of Greenhouse Gases," CNN, updated December 9, 2020, https://www.cnn.com/2019/06/03/world/gallery/surprising-sources-greenhouse-gas-emissions-intl/index.html.

the question of environmental impact. Is making a lithium battery for two billion cars going to cause us more damage or good? What about the carbon production to train an AI model?

Regulatory and Legal Pressure

A series of climate-based lawsuits against big oil companies began coming to trial in 2023—a form of pressure to adapt.[52]

And in the coming years, large public companies are going to be required to report on the carbon impact of their supply chain and their suppliers. The "peer pressure" side of this is going to be massive.

If your company engages with a transportation provider that is using 10 times the carbon compared to their competitor, and you have to report on that and pay for additional carbon credits, that's going to become a huge sticking point—hard dollars are at stake.

I think we're going to see more and more of that punitive environmental legislation coming out—because we simply won't be able to ignore it: as I write this, five of the hottest days in the past 125,000 years have occurred within the last 30 days.[53] Don't look up.

If you had a usage-based billing and rating system in place, had the telemetry of your manufacturing supply and sales chain, and understood that a truck driving a load of widgets one mile created X carbon, then, in the usage system, you could track each one of the

52 "Climate Litigation More Than Doubles in Five Years, Now a Key Tool in Delivering Climate Justice," UN Environment Programme, July 27, 2023, https://www.unep.org/news-and-stories/press-release/climate-litigation-more-doubles-five-years-now-key-tool-delivering.
53 Andrew Freedman, "The 15 Hottest Days, in the World's Hottest Month," Axios, July 20, 2023, https://www.axios.com/2023/07/20/world-heat-wave-records-us-europe-china.

miles travelled by each truck and its weight, rate it a carbon charge, and then buy a credit or report on that—or even dump a vendor who was generating too much carbon cost.

Without the technological capacity to have that atomic-level counting of the events within your supply chain, and without knowing what the carbon production of each of those events was, I don't know how any company would, with a straight face, report on those forthcoming carbon-disclosure requirements.

The ratification of this legislation would be a sledgehammer! You think a businessperson wouldn't be motivated to keep themselves out of jail? Or to ensure their company continues to get projects?

But that reporting can't be satisfied unless you have the capacity to understand the usage within your supply chain and then assign carbon charges to it.

Some companies have begun taking these steps independent of legislation. Singapore-based Giti Tire Group aimed to calculate emissions related to standard passenger tires produced by a subsidiary, PTGT. So, it worked with its suppliers and relied on publicly available emissions factors and identified the major emissions sources—and, after gathering the data, the company considered how it could reduce emissions.[54]

Suppliers, similarly, began proposing emissions-reducing alternatives.

---

54 Robert S. Kaplan, Karthik Ramanna, and Stefan J. Reichelstein, "Getting a Clearer View of Your Company's Carbon Footprint," *HBR*, April 3, 2023, https://hbr.org/2023/04/getting-a-clearer-view-of-your-companys-carbon-footprint.

Looking Ahead

With every piece of telemetry, there is an opportunity to either save or make money.

Once you have that data, you can step in to solve a problem.

Whether it's cost savings or new ways of being able to price and sell your products, opportunities abound—but it's all contingent on the underlying data.

///

KEY CHAPTER TAKEAWAYS

→ Regardless of where you stand on environmental issues, they will be front and centre for future generations.

→ Usage and sharing models can benefit the environment even when the product's or service's main goals aren't environmentally focused.

→ Looking at things at the atomic level forces companies to consider supply chain costs and inefficiencies.

08/ TECHNOLOGICAL

TECH DEVELOPMENTS ARE DRIVING USAGE-BASED INNOVA-tions—it's the underlying thread connecting the Usage Economy.

We use so many devices today, and we stand poised to develop so many more. Wearables. Avalanche beacons. Satellite phones. There's even the potential of services like Starlink internet, which provides internet coverage to more than 50 countries through a sea of satellites.

How far off are we from a pervasive satellite internet network where we no longer need to bury fibre or copper infrastructure in the ground at huge capital expense?

Our telecommunications networks are costly. Satellites are way more cost-effective with way better coverage.[55]

What would happen if there were such a pervasive network—one global network owned by a huge company—and we were all on it, whether it were a computer in California, a phone in Tanzania, a

---

55 Neel V. Patel, "Here's How Just Four Satellites Could Provide Worldwide Internet," MIT, January 16, 2020, https://www.technologyreview.com/2020/01/16/130832/heres-how-just-four-satellites-could-provide-worldwide-internet/.

connected watch in South Africa, or a beacon in Canada?

How would you charge for that? Who would fund it? How would it be maintained and by whom? How would it be monetized? These are the issues we'll have to confront as we continue to see consolidation of investment in high tech.

Cloud Computing

We're seeing the deployment of cloud computing models by leading cloud service providers like Amazon Web Services, Microsoft Azure, and Google Cloud. They promise their customers that these models will offset and change the risk profiles of the way companies bring products to market.

These vendors want companies to make a commitment to paying for services. But if they charge $80 million up front, that's a heavy financial burden. If they put the money in a bucket and just draw it down based on usage as services are used, that's a lot more digestible. That way, a company doesn't have to have its engineering team go off and guess how much it will spend discretely on RAM and CPUs and storage before bringing their product to market. The commitment can be spent in infinite variety across the vendor's catalogue.

Data Collection and Analysis

The information we're now able to gather due to sensors and IoT products is changing the scope of what we can quantify and monetize.

It's possible now to collect data on manhole covers and the number of times they're impacted by cars driving over them—which is help-ful for understanding when to swap them out. It's also possible to detect potholes. As the car is travelling over a roadway, it can now gather and send back data on the condition of the road, and through mapping software, it can tell us exactly where potholes are located.

Speed of traffic is one we've embraced—if you take a look at Google Maps, they're taking all the telematics from Android phones with Google Maps installed on them and sending that data back to show traffic patterns. There's so much data running through vehicles right now—and so many ways to utilize or monetize it.

Security and Privacy

People are becoming increasingly aware of regulations and best practices around data privacy—and businesses need to act accordingly.

Consider Facebook, which faced reputational damage due to its mishandling of data privacy. It was forced to pay $1.3 billion by European Union investigators and agreed to settle a class action lawsuit in the United States for $725 million.[56]

Customers are becoming more and more savvy about their information and how it's stored and used. And companies are going to need to adapt.

Example: Car Insurance

I recently received a call from my car insurance company.

"We wanted to let you know that your make and model of car has a high risk of theft potential," the caller told me.

---

56 Kelvin Chan, "European Union Fines Facebook Parent Meta 390M Euros for Privacy Violations," PBS News Hour, January 4, 2023, https://www.pbs.org/newshour/world/european-union-fines-facebook-parent-meta-390m-euros-for-privacy-violations.

"OK, thanks for letting me know," I said.

"Well, actually, sir, you will have the option of a $400 surcharge annually, or we will install a GPS tracker on your car so that if it is stolen, we have a higher chance of recovering it."

Um ... the insurance company's alternative to colleting my GPS data was a punitive $400 fee?! There were thousands of ways they could have better presented this situation to me. It got the hair on the back of my neck standing up because it felt as if I was being extorted—they wanted me to pay up or let them track my vehicle. I wasn't even sure if the GPS unit they wanted to install was active or passive—I was already "on alert."

"There's absolutely no way that an insurance company is installing any tracking anything in anything I own, ever, for any reason," I said. "I'll go get a quote for a new insurance company. I am interested, however, in seeing all the paperwork surrounding this initiative. I want to understand what you're going to do with the data from the tracker in my car, how it's going to be stored, whether it's passive or active, when and how it is activated, what your data protection agreement will be with me as a consumer, whether you will sell my data—I want to understand how this works." I was genuinely interested, not as a customer, but as someone whose career is focused on usage-based models.

"Nobody's asked us for that," the customer service rep said.

If the situation had been presented as an opportunity for a discount if I installed the tracking system—or even if I'd just been informed that my premium was increasing because theft rates were up due to a rough economy—I'm sure I would have felt much differently.

As more of these types of models become pervasive, when every commercial entity you interact with is going to be collecting lots of usage data, security and privacy are going to draw more and more attention, and customers and vendors alike are going to become savvier.

Companies that protect customer data will be celebrated; those that fail to respect local laws or just look to sell customer data will be called out and denigrated. My insurance company—which stands to benefit from selling my data—approached me in what I perceived to be a distasteful manner and failed to explain how I would benefit from their gathering my information (or whether they would be gathering information); they only explained that it would save me some money.

And as a result of that call, after being a customer for 20 years, I found a new insurance company.

Blockchain

Money is fake, and it doesn't mean anything—not since it stopped being tied to the gold standard. There's nothing backing it up except for our belief in the fiat system.

Governments print trillions of dollars at a time, and the national debts continue to skyrocket, and it's all just brushed aside. It's a dangerous drug, knowing you can run your own printing press whenever you want to pay your bills. But each time you do it, the value of your dollar diminishes.

If your debt-to-income ratio was like the government's, as a private human being, you wouldn't be approved for credit anywhere, anytime, for any reason. But it's perfectly acceptable to operate that way as a nation-state.

It feels obvious that there are some shenanigans going on in our capital markets, which are increasing the need for regulation and transparency. Something is wrong when people can't afford food or shelter, yet trillions get sucked out the top of the funnel, to the detriment of most of society, with no visibility into how money is moving.

How long until change is demanded, and what might that change look like?

Some elements of blockchain—in which transactions are stored and recorded in a decentralized ledger that everyone can see—could present a solution. Given the transparency, the blockchain data ties in strongly to usage-based models.

The Emerging Frontier

Any talk of technology would be incomplete without highlighting the emerging frontier of AI.

AI represents the future of the Usage Economy and provides perspective into what a connected world looks like. It's a fascinating thing to think about. But it comes with lots of considerations, risks, and opportunities.

///

KEY CHAPTER TAKEAWAYS

→   Tech developments are driving usage-based innovations and fuelling the Usage Economy.

→   The information we're now able to gather due to sensors and

IoT products is changing the scope of what we can quantify and monetize.

→ People are becoming increasingly aware of regulation and best practices around data privacy—and businesses need to act accordingly.

09/ AI

ARTIFICIAL INTELLIGENCE HAS EVERYBODY'S ATTENTION these days.

McKinsey & Company published a telling article in March 2023 called "Actions the Best CEOs Are Taking in 2023," which looked at executives' priorities and actions. CEOs identified disruptive technology—such as AI—as the year's most important trend, being named by 58% of survey participants. AI scored above the economy (56%) and geopolitics (47%).

As one responder wrote, "A CEO also has to be the chief technology architect. Think of the executive team—not just the chief digital officer—as owning the technology strategy of the company. There is too much at stake."[57]

Artificial intelligence—in particular generative large language models like ChatGPT—has accelerated business transformation by

---

57 Carolyn Dewar, Scott Keller, Vikram Malhotra, and Kurt Strovink, "Actions the Best CEOs Are Taking in 2023," McKinsey & Company, March 15, 2023, https://www.mckinsey.com/capabilities/strategy-and-corporate-finance/our-insights/actions-the-best-ceos-are-taking-in-2023.

changing the way we access and interpret data. It revolutionizes the way that we can get prospect or customer information to tailor our go-to-market efforts.

Previously, gathering all that data that isn't just searchable or retrievable from a vendor's database would take thousands of hours of human effort. Now, though, it's literally dollars' worth of AI tokens, digital assets that can be used to purchase goods and services.

If you want to get a piece of content, you can buy a few tokens, and they are consumed as you create prompts. The amount of computing power and resources that are deployed to support a platform like ChatGPT are astronomical—so we can almost count on an evolution of a usage-based model that will contemplate the complexity of the query, analyze the collective texts of humanity, and recommend the best way to get rid of that bump on your pinky finger, versus delivering a simple response, which doesn't require a lot of context or computation, like the time of day.

Today, those queries both consume one token, but surely that will evolve in the near future.

Hundreds of billions of dollars will be freed up due to AI as companies increase their efficiency and scale, and it's going to be a race to grab those dollars.

Business is competition. And if you're neglecting the hundreds of billions of dollars up for grabs by failing to automate your operations and systems, you're going to be at a massive disadvantage relative to your competition.

The New Usage-Based World

In the context of the usage-based world, a company faces lots of questions as it brings a product or service to market regarding price, sales model, markets, and target demographic.

In the case of digital and connected services in particular, those services generate a massive amount of extremely valuable usage telemetry—showing how often the product was interacted with, when, how, how long it was used, whether it was in compliance with the customer's prepaid plan, what APIs were being called, the power that was consumed, the flow rate ... and on and on and on.

Where billing is concerned, once you've collected all that information, you can break things down to the basic elements. You can measure how much a kilobyte of kilowatt costs, or the price of an updated marine map, or the cost to send a ping to a satellite network when you need a rescue. When you break things all the way down, you can assign charges accordingly.

When you do that, and bill the customer, you'll have a wealth of information around the billing process:

→   How quickly did you collect your money from the customer?
→   How long did it take them to pay after they saw the invoice?
→   What percentage of those invoices or charges were refuted?
→   How many customers renewed?
→   What was your churn rate?
→   What was your growth rate?
→   In what season or time of day were products purchased?

Once you have this wealth of information, you can do something with it. And that's what the new usage-based world looks like.

In the context of AI, it far surpasses the capability of a human brain or team of human brains using a traditional reporting mechanism to identify patterns and extract correlations. And even if it's not perfect yet, it's going to improve quickly. The more information we feed it, the better it will get.

No More Guesswork

Systems like ChatGPT are great at gathering general information about the internet and humanity. Watching every YouTube video, reading every internet page, and devouring every book isn't feasible for anyone—or even a team of people—but this information is being used to build out AI datasets.

With the right dataset, what might AI technology reveal about your business? About your products and customers? What questions could it answer that are beyond the scope of human calculation and correlation?

Uncovering better models for a company's go-to-market or reducing churn or developing meaningful bundles to sell to customers currently amounts to guesswork.

But AI will soon have the ability to observe these correlations and make these recommendations to generate the content that is being prompted from it.

The next phase of artificial intelligence will involve the capacity to collect all this telemetry and transform it into a dataset that can be appropriately consumed by an AI to tune it on the specifics of your business, your customers, your devices, your APIs, your usage, your telemetry, and all the other glorious detail that will really help to make these AI systems smart—and take a company to new heights.

100 Million Brains Working Together

Our opinions about how to run a company are guided by a mix of industry standards, best practices, individual style, and personal experiences. Maybe you do things a certain way because it worked before. Or maybe you just prefer things that certain way.

But the ideas and suggestions generated by AI are based entirely on the data consumed. It doesn't have any personal pride or stake in the game.

For example, there are ways to increase your revenue by combining products you probably haven't considered or other types of offerings that your customers may prefer. You may be able to implement a pricing strategy that your customers will love. You may slice and dice your reports a certain way. But AI is like 100 million human brains working on this all at once, cohesively coming together with the same opinion on the other end.

Uncovering the Unknowable

Consider two companies—company A and company B.

Company A doesn't invest in AI technology. The company doesn't see the point. It's been successful for a long time.

Company B has a well-trained AI process, and it may be taking actions based on recommendations unknowable by human beings.

Even if company A has an employee base of really smart people, how are they going to compete with the AI-driven actions of company B?

It is a very small proportion of businesses that can be successful and not technologically focused nowadays. Even the tractor sowing the fields is connected to GPS and is capable of self-driving and is monitoring yields, seeding density, and moisture content, while predicting germination rates.

Businesses that embrace these developments can expect exponential growth. Companies that are flying blind on all this information are effectively turning their backs on all the collective knowledge of humanity as revealed by AI and large language models. The competitive bar has never been set higher.

Unbiased Truths

Humans are unpredictable beings. And what we perceive to be true is often not. So AI with telemetry on your interactions will either prove your instincts to be true or show you another, better way that you may not have otherwise considered.

You may not have a good reason for disliking something.

Surveys are inaccurate. People might be nicer—or meaner—than they should be, or they may misremember or be having a bad day. We're fickle creatures who are skewed by the emotions of the moment.

Even if you've sold a product, you may never be able to successfully solicit feedback from customers. They buy it and walk away, then get an invitation to fill out a survey. "Yeah, right," they say.

But usage data, on the other hand, is not skewed by emotions.

AI doesn't need a survey—it doesn't have biases. It's not trying to protect anyone's feelings. It's not prone to a predisposition of self-image that would manipulate behaviour or true wants or desires. It will just look at the mathematics of how your behaviour shows that you are interacting and provide you an objective and analytical prediction, or it will answer with how that human will behave and what that human wants.

As humans, we're predisposed and programmed. When someone asks how we're doing, we say "fine," even when we're not. Nobody actually wants to hear an answer to that question.

But if you were to observe someone's behaviour—they arrive for coffee 30 minutes later than their usual time, and they order a higher-caffeinated coffee, and the telemetry from their car shows they stopped in the middle of the roadway, indicating a traffic jam or a flat tire—then you could probably predict based on those and a number of other data points how that person's day was going, whether it is actually going well or not.

Social conventions are so familiar to us, but gathering information based on actual telemetry is so much more valuable and accurate.

One of the capabilities that I've found interesting is the ability of an AI, based on signal reception in a roomful of Wi-Fi, to create a 3D map of that room just by observing the bouncing of the radio signals.[58] And in the same way that I can postulate the terrain of a room and its occupants through signals bouncing around in the air, so too should I be able to paint a picture of human behaviour based on the

---

58 Andrew Liszewski, "The Invisible Radio Waves All Around Us Let MIT's New AI See People Right Through Walls," Gizmodo, June 13, 2018, https://gizmodo.com/the-invisible-radio-waves-all-around-us-let-mits-new-ai-1826794669.

telemetry that surrounds them.

That raises all sorts of competitive, innovative, and ethical questions.

If I'm able to predict what you're going to do before you do it, what does marketing regulation look like?

Travel and AI

One of our team members was recently planning a vacation.

Typically, you'd Google to find hotels and attractions and shopping and restaurants and manually plan your trip based on user reviews and insights. That process could take days or weeks. And you're left wondering if that 4.5 rating is something you should worry about.

Instead, the team member input their interests and goals into ChatGPT and developed an itinerary. And within seconds, they had an itinerary based off 100 million points of data gathered over the internet.

The itinerary required some fine-tuning and double-checking, but not much.

You may think your industry or market penetration is impenetrable, that you've covered every risk and capitalized on every opportunity—but have you?

The Ultimate Question

In *The Hitchhiker's Guide to the Galaxy* by British sci-fi author Douglas Adams, there's a computer known as Deep Thought, and Deep Thought knows everything. Two of the characters ask Deep Thought for the answer to life, the universe, and everything :

Fook composed himself.

"O Deep Thought computer," he said, "the task we have designed you to perform is this. We want you to tell us ..." he paused, "the Answer!"

"The Answer?" said Deep Thought. "The Answer to what?"

"Life!" urged Fook.

"The Universe!" said Lunkwill.

"Everything!" they said in chorus.

Deep Thought paused for a moment's reflection.

"Tricky," he said finally.

"But can you do it?"

Again, a significant pause.

"Yes," said Deep Thought, "I can do it."

"There is an answer?" said Fook with breathless excitement.

"A simple answer?" added Lunkwill.

"Yes," said Deep Thought. "Life, the Universe and Everything. There is an answer. But," he added, "I'll have to think about it." [59]

Deep Thought's eventual answer is "42."

---

59 Douglas Adams, *The Hitchhiker's Guide to the Galaxy* (New York: Harmony Books, 1980).

With AI, as with Deep Thought, the relevance of the answer is contingent on the understanding of question you're asking.

As AI continues to advance, there are things that will increasingly be automated—making a PowerPoint, drawing a picture, writing a brochure, chatting on the customer support line. The human practice will increasingly become asking the right question.

To a system that knows everything, from a dataset so large, it's crucial to be specific and provide the right context to get a relevant answer. In the AI world, this is known as prompt engineering, or tuning, depending on the approach.

We're all going to be tasked with becoming prompt engineers. And asking the right question is how you can extract meaning from life, the universe, AI, and everything.

The answers are all available. It's a matter of knowing what to ask.

If you could ask AI anything—about your business and financial model and usage data—what would you ask? What would you want to know?

Therein lies the difficulty—or the opportunity.

Example: Five9

The software company Five9, a leading global contact centre provider, has been using AI in innovative ways.

Its intelligent virtual-agent chatbots can help with repetitive, easy tasks, freeing up human agents to handle more complex tasks while reducing costs for companies.

Five9's Agent Assist 2.0 with AI Summary, powered by OpenAI—the maker of ChatGPT—summarizes customer-call transcripts in seconds, reducing manual busy after-call reporting and freeing up agents to work better and faster.

This kind of process also takes the guesswork out of call agents' reports and ensures that nothing is missed.

All this AI works in tandem with Five9's usage-based billing platform.[60] Every touchpoint has been designed with efficiency—and the potential to scale—in mind.

AI Risks

Despite so much potential surrounding AI, there are also risks, especially involving data.

OpenAI faced a wave of lawsuits in mid-2023 over the accusation that the AI was trained on publicly available information without the consent of people publishing the content, as well as issues around copyright or data privacy requirements.[61]

In one lawsuit, authors Paul Tremblay and Mona Awad claimed that ChatGPT's precise summaries of their works were only possible if it was trained on their books.[62] A proposed class action lawsuit was

---

60 Suzie Linville, "Five9 Introduces Agent Assist 2.0 with AI Summary Powered by OpenAI," Five9, March 28, 2023, https://investors.five9.com/news-releases/news-release-details/five9-introduces-agent-assist-20-ai-summary-powered-openai.

61 Cassandre Coyer, "OpenAI Is Getting Sued. Legal Tech Vendors Using Their Generative AI Models Aren't Worried," Law.com, August 17, 2023, https://www.law.com/legaltechnews/2023/08/17/openai-is-getting-sued-legal-tech-vendors-using-their-generative-ai-models-arent-worried/.

62 Alexandra Tremayne-Pengelly, "Mona Awad and Paul Tremblay Are the Latest Creatives to Sue Over A.I.," *Observer*, August 7, 2023, https://observer.com/2023/07/mona-awad-paul-tremblay-sue-chatgpt-copyright-infringement/.

filed in California, while leading media organizations were weighing legal action of their own.

The text generated from AI like ChatGPT doesn't include attribution. If you are going to train an AI from the fount of a billion minds, you would really need molecular economics in order to properly compensate and attribute sources of content in a massive language model with a complex set of training data, licensed under many different conditions from a multitude of sources.

We have so many expectations around AI. We want it to be this omnipotent, Deep Thought–level knowledge base trained on the collective knowledge of humanity but then also cite and verify the discrete sources across the entire dataset from which it forms a suggestion.

If ChatGPT makes an inference that turns out to be of value, based on training data that you put on the internet that's copyrighted, are you then entitled to a share of OpenAI's revenue?

How would you prove it?

Just imagine the unforeseen complexity if someone gets a fraction of revenue for every question asked that relies on your dataset as a response basis.

At LogiSense, our policy is to not post any private information into any of these public AI systems. It's fine to go spend a few tokens and have a piece of content created for you, but we do not post code or confidential information into them. And we don't use AI in any other cases except for output unless the person has approval from a company executive.

We still need to understand the exact agreements in terms of data protection, anti-intellectual property protection, and how the information may or may not be used in terms of a future training set for a commercial version of that AI.

We don't fully understand yet how to use it for mission-critical functions. And we still see some variances in the performance of these systems, like the concept of AI hallucination, where it will create content to provide you the answer that you're looking for. And it's capable of doing that or generating other unpredictable behaviours. In terms of leaving it to do things like contract authoring or book writing, it still requires human intervention.

The Great Unknown

One of our customers is exploring the possibility of having AI do audits on their billing data when they know they're going to be audited, since they're a public company.

That way, they can get ahead of the auditor and pick up things that might need to be addressed ahead of time. Such tools could help them automate and reduce time, effort, and cost.

Other companies are focused on using AI for sales and marketing efforts.

But AI still represents a great unknown.

Data security is a huge obstacle of artificial intelligence, in particular with GDPR in Europe and Privacy Shield,[63] and the fines can be significant. If you're found to be misbehaving, the costs are steep.

---

63 "European Union - Data Privacy and Protection," Privacy Shield Framework, accessed November 1, 2023, https://www.privacyshield.gov/ps/article?id=European-Union-Data-Privatization-and-Protection.

An AI-Aided Future

It's an interesting thought exercise to imagine an easier life with some sort of assistant that knows your preferences and has access to your personal records and data. It reminds you when to take your pills and starts the coffee maker when you're nearing home from your morning jog because you typically have your coffee when you settle in.

That kind of life is only possible with proprietary telemetry paired with a real-time dataset.

The more we consider the way technologies evolve from devices to services, the more that products and services become software themselves—accessing the internet, ordering online, receiving service help online, finding the user manual online, sharing commentary and connecting with like-minded users online, and gathering data around those interactions.

All those interactions and touchpoints represent golden opportunities.

The more you invest in the infrastructure to harvest that telemetry and make use of it, the more that virtual circle of go-to-market telemetry, billing, collecting revenue, analysis, refinement, and go-back-to-market will get faster and sharper—and eventually will start creating products all on its own.

The company that created the medium widget could roll out the ultra-sized widget with a demographic already pinpointed, and they would know it will cost $250,000 to go to market, and the publicly available market data suggests that the company could make $10 million.

How exciting would that be?

New Data = New Opportunities

Emerging technologies are going to create new opportunities to track, quantify, and monitor information—which is only going to lead to more incentives to consider usage-based models.

More things that we currently can't track will be trackable.

In the next section, we consider the "how" of usage-based transactions—implementation and results.

//

KEY CHAPTER TAKEAWAYS

→ Artificial intelligence has accelerated business transformation by changing the way we access and interpret data.

→ If you're neglecting the chance to automate your operations and systems, you're going to be at a massive disadvantage relative to your competition.

→ Despite so much potential surrounding AI, there are also risks, especially involving data.

IMPLEMENTATION AND RESULTS

This is where the rubber meets the road.

The following chapters detail steps and tips to consider when shifting your company to a usage-based model.

10/ CHALLENGES TO IMPLEMENTATION

THE SHIFT TO USAGE-BASED TRANSACTIONS IS UNIQUE FOR every company.

It's a chance to rethink everything—to reimagine the business and its offerings. When considering taking a leap, business owners need to take a lot of factors into account, including revenue, pricing, risk, the way the company treats its customers, and the approach to infrastructure and technology.

Revenue

A 2020 study by TechCrunch revealed that year-over-year revenue growth was up 38% for public SaaS companies that employed usage-based pricing models over those that didn't.[64] As Kyle Poyar wrote for TechCrunch, "Public SaaS companies that have adopted

---

64 Kyle Poyar, "Why Do SaaS Companies with Usage-Based Pricing Grow Faster?" TechCrunch, February 18, 2021, https://techcrunch.com/2021/02/18/why-do-saas-companies-with-usage-based-pricing-grow-faster/.

usage-based pricing grow faster because they're better at landing new customers, growing with them and keeping them as customers."

But in order to capture that revenue, companies need to know their business and customers—what they value and the coveted value metrics—and use that understanding to properly price their products and services.

It's crucial for companies to consider historical sales data when making that shift. Key metrics to consider include the following:

→ Annual recurring revenue (ARR)
→ Monthly recurring revenue (MRR)
→ Customer lifetime value (CLV)
→ Customer acquisition costs (CAC)
→ Customer churn rate

As far as I'm aware, there is no silver bullet in creating an algorithm from which to derive perfect insight into these types of metrics. There is hope that AI can deliver that, insofar as it develops algorithms that we don't understand—but there are the basics of tracking this information.

There's a number of different data science or business intelligence practices that companies can use to glean insight from key metrics by plugging data into a reporting or business intelligence framework like Tableau or Qlik or Snowflake or Databricks.

At this stage, you also need a smart and sophisticated group of people to develop the math or the right set of reporting to get insight from those raw metrics—people who can take these metrics and create correlations or recognize patterns or behaviours.

For example, if every time ARR increases due to a baseline annual uplift, you experience a 6% uptick in churn within 30 to 60 days among your customer base—it probably means that people don't like the big uplift delivered all at once. Is there a better way to deliver that uplift in smaller portions monthly as an additional upsell or package?

Finding those correlations and then determining the cause is an art and a science, but you need the right people with the right skill sets and experience to be able to do that effectively.

Not every company has the resources to employ and attract a roomful of people to properly crunch the data—not every company is like NASA or Amazon. In time, AI will be tapped to make correlations and uncover patterns, which will help to level the playing field.

A rising tide lifts all boats, and as these technologies become more accessible, companies will be better equipped to uncover revenue patterns and position their services for growth.

Pricing Strategy

The transition or addition of usage-based models can look a lot like educated guesses to a business owner today. Maybe customers have asked for a wider range of product or service offerings, or the owner thinks there is untapped revenue potential.

Very soon, we're going to start to see a broader adoption of customized AI models that help to inform that process.

Usage data or telemetry is at the core of product design. And if you don't have access to your usage data, or an AI engine, it requires you to go back to the basics and ask the important questions:

108 /// THE USAGE ECONOMY

→ What are our objectives as a business?

→ What are the objectives around our product?

→ Is retention more important than adoption?

→ Is growth more important than everything else?

→ Is profit more important than everything else?

Start to think about pricing your product. Think about how your customers perceive your product, and identify the value metric around which you want to construct your go-to-market pricing (more on this in Chapter 12). Then you'll do all the normal financial functions and modelling to ensure that that will be consistent with revenue expectations.

Risk

It's impossible to anticipate every risk factor your company will face, especially in volatile times. Life-altering events like the stock market crash, coronavirus pandemic, and housing bubble can't always be anticipated. And, as a result, it's not always clear when customer habits will change.

Relying on the usage telemetry your company has gathered—along with advanced analytics tools and AI models—can help predict usage trends and diminish a company's risk.

Everything starts with information and analysis. Machine learning and AI can be used to detect usage patterns, from peak seasonality to infrastructure needs. The best predictor of retention for software is log-ins—people using your product. If they aren't using your product, it's only a matter of time before they consider cancelling their service.

Until relatively recently, we didn't have the infrastructural capability to be able to collect and consolidate that telemetry for processing. But today, we do.

Spectrum of Models

We've previously addressed how every transaction model has corresponding risk factors, with risk shifting between seller and buyer based on the type of transaction.

In between those poles of traditional one-time transactions and pure usage-based consumption billing is a spectrum of numerous other models. Sometimes purchases come with an ongoing annuity—that used to be the way hardware was sold. In the 1980s and 1990s, the concept of hardware was ordering a big Sun Microsystems server. It would come with a maintenance annuity that you'd pay every year. The power supply would burn out, then a technician would come out with a new power supply and install it.

Then you started to graduate into the traditional perpetual software sale, where you have a one-time licensing entitlement—you then own the licence to that software—and with a maintenance annuity alongside it, you can get upgraded to more recent versions of the software and have somebody answer the phone when you have an issue. A one-time sale of the intellectual property and then an ongoing support and maintenance annuity has evolved into subscriptions.

Even subscriptions have a spectrum and a balance of risk. A multi-year contract was much less risky to a vendor who had to purchase servers and deploy them in the pre-cloud era. For the customer, everything was included in one flat price.

A big multi-year contract might be totally appropriate for enterprise software, but you might not want to agree to five years with Netflix—you don't know what the quality of their catalogue is going to look like. It makes more sense to go month to month, and that puts more risk on the vendor. The vendor has to ensure that there is continual value delivered to the consumer, or the customer can cancel that subscription with only a 30-day penalty.

If the customer were charged in arrears on exactly what they consumed, all the risk would be with the vendor providing the service—and if you have a prepaid model, it shifts the risk back to the consumer.

Finding the Right Plan

As you move from the traditional one-time transaction model into usage, you have the potential to reduce sales cycles to make it easier to onboard customers to drive more growth and to be competitive via the commercial model itself.

Without heavy upfront charges, and with payments based on usage, the risk shifts from the consumer to the vendor. But vendors get the benefit of decreased time cycles. And this applies in different ways to different industries.

It's not always appropriate to charge in a pure usage way, because that might not fit your risk appetite. Maybe it's more beneficial for you if you have some sunk costs to establish a basic subscription with the usage component—a combination of the two—or to implement more of a multi-year term, or to implement something that reduces risk on both ends of the spectrum by moving to a prepaid drawdown type of model. In that kind of model, the capital is set aside, and you can use any number of products and services to spend that capital.

Minimum-commitment plans that combine fixed and variable fees can reduce the unknowns that come with forecasting future revenue.

Customer Relationship

One of the tricky parts with usage-based models is the learning curve for customers.

They may not know how much data or how many resources they use each month or year, meaning they might not have a good idea of how much money they will spend each month. Expensive overages for the customer are possible.

Using prepaid allotments can help reassure customers. Maybe the customer is paying for a web service on an API basis, and the pricing model involves variable tokens that cover a fraction of a cent per token—but given the variable cost, it's tough to gauge how much they will use of the service. The buyer can use a credit card with a capped amount on it, or potentially, they set up daily or monthly usage caps that will alert them if they are exceeding usage and, therefore, cost thresholds. Those checks and guardrails can help ensure that a customer isn't overspending and facing runaway charges on their credit card because some script had a wrong loop in it.

Retention

Usage data, if properly crunched and analyzed, can help you reduce churn by engaging customers more efficiently and diminishing pain points.

In one LogiSense survey, 54% of CFOs agreed that having a usage-based option could reduce customer churn.[65] For companies offering a subscription service, their traditional plans typically aren't a fit for every customer—and being able to have flexible, usage-based options is a great way to keep customers satisfied and engaged.

If it's mid-month and a customer is hardly using a service, or they are on pace to exceed their service threshold and are on track to face overage charges, a usage-based option gives companies an opportunity to engage customers at that point and upsell them to a larger commitment: "You're over the usage where you should be right now. Have you thought about changing to a plan that better suits your usage? Under your current plan, you'd actually pay more than if you switched to this different plan." Or it just gives them a chance to give them a head's up and keep them informed—driving increased loyalty and a better experience, retention, and lifetime value.

It may seem counterproductive to proactively offer your customers discounts, but it's a fantastic option from a customer-loyalty perspective. And it pays off in the long run. It's better to treat them fairly, getting them paying a proper rate for the products and services they use and establishing strong customer loyalty, rather than milking them until they wise up and cancel their service. It costs a lot more to acquire a dollar of new-customer business than to sell an additional dollar to an existing customer.

Having that visibility and those triggers gives you an opportunity to provide that customer service before the person gets the disap-

---

65 LogiSense (@LogiSense), "Did you know? 54% of CFOs surveyed by LogiSense agree that introducing flexible 'pay-as-you-use' pricing can be a game-changer in reducing customer churn!," X (formerly Twitter), May 15, 2023, 12:07 p.m., https://twitter.com/LogiSense/status/1658172144566583296.

pointment of seeing their bill. And it shows them loyalty. A company that's not looking to pull every last cent out of their pockets—but that's giving them a good experience and value for the money they're spending—is more likely to retain the customer and improve their lifetime value, retention, opportunity for upsell, and customer experience.

Maintaining a current customer is much cheaper than having to find and convert a new lead.

Infrastructure and Technology

There are other challenges to implementation, too, that are necessary to resolve. Your company's infrastructure and operations need to be able to evolve and to handle large usage spikes. Without being able to safely, securely track and collect usage data, your company is limited by what it can offer or accomplish and how it can take products to market.

There is a balance with data privacy and security—collecting the right data without collecting too much data or data that may unduly put your organization at risk. Misuse data or collect too much of it, and a company is liable to face stiff penalties or increase their exposure in the event of a breach.

Underneath it all, there needs to be a billing and data-transformation engine, a chance for customers to be able to monitor and track their own usage.

Evolution

The shift from traditional to usage-based transactions is going to evolve in the coming years.

My company is currently evaluating the development of an online tool where you can simulate an economic model based on your company's actual data. So you could have a baseline, traditional-model company, and against it, you can simulate a usage-based future where product A is sold as a consumption drawdown but with products B, C, and D on top of that.

Trying out a simulation can give companies the confidence to proceed where they normally would have held firm.

Being able to take five years of usage telemetry for retention, product usage, consumption location, customer details, you name it, and letting the AI engine predict what the correlations are across this huge dataset will help you achieve the perfect model and price point.

Think of it: taking a dataset that's so large, it's beyond the scope of human knowability, one that could take years for a team of people to synthesize and review—and instead having it reviewed in a matter of moments.

The fundamentals of this start with pricing, followed by product design and understanding your market and your company's risk tolerance and priorities, identifying the key value metric, and then modelling what that might look like compared to what your business looks like today.

It's an awesome thing.

///

KEY CHAPTER TAKEAWAYS

→ The shift to usage-based transactions is a chance to reimagine your business and its offerings.

→ Relying on the usage telemetry your company has gathered—along with advanced analytics tools and AI models—can help predict usage trends and diminish a company's risk.

→ As you move from the traditional one-time transaction model into usage, you have the potential to reduce sales cycles to make it easier to onboard customers to drive more growth and to be competitive via the commercial model itself.

11 / GRANULARITY AND FLEXIBILITY

THERE ARE MORE THAN 200,000 POSSIBLE WAYS TO ORDER A Burger King Whopper, as the fast-food chain highlighted in a 2023 marketing campaign.[66] That's a lot of different combinations for a simple sandwich!

Some people order their Whoppers with extra crunch (pickles), spice (jalapeños), or tang (BBQ sauce). Some order their sandwiches with two or three patties. Others order plant-based Impossible Whopper sandwiches.[67]

All those preferences and inputs help to provide a personalized customer experience. Your sandwich won't taste exactly like the next person's. Maybe the chain's long-time slogan, "Have it your way," has some truth to it.

---

66 "A Flame-Grilled 'State' of Mind: Americans Unite on Their Love for the Whopper®" Business Wire, May 23, 2023, https://www.businesswire.com/news/home/20230523005395/en/A-Flame-Grilled-'State'-of-Mind-Americans-Unite-on-Their-Love-for-the-Whopper.

67 "A Flame-Grilled 'State' of Mind: Americans Unite on Their Love for the Whopper."

The Usage Economy works similarly. Atomic-level transactions offer customers ultimate freedom to pursue creative solutions to their needs—which in turn drives customer satisfaction and expansion. Granularity and flexibility are tantamount to the Usage Economy and go hand in hand.

Granularity and Customer Engagement

Historically, we haven't been able to look at economic motion at any level of granularity. The amount of data gleaned from a traditional one-time sale is very limited.

The old model came with a lot of guesswork. Companies would try five new things and continue the one that worked.

But atomic-level economics is really about being technologically enabled enough to ingest this telemetry and understand every interaction the customer has had with the product, the product's life cycle, and whether the customer is engaged with the product.

If a customer buys a $500 smartwatch and activates it for two months then stops using it, that's a chance to get in contact with the customer. Ask them, "Is there anything we can help you with? Is there anything wrong with the device?" If customers are disengaging with a product, that's an indication that it's time to make an improvement in the services you're delivering and drive more adoption—focusing on creating more value, driving more sign-ups, and retaining more customers.

Deal Complexity

Granularity is all about tailoring a deal to an enterprise—and with usage-based models, the sales process can be as simple or complex as the mind imagines.

A salesperson can dream up any model to close the deal. Maybe it involves devices and getting the customer to buy 50,000 devices—but they don't want them all at once. They want 1,000 devices deployed for 50 months, locked in at a $50,000 a month price.

There are all these negotiations around rollouts and ramp-ups, and the pricing is deal-specific and complex.

With deal complexity and flexibility, the issue becomes enforcing these contracts and staying on top of them.

Everything has to be correct so the customer is satisfied that what they bought is in line with the products and services they are being provided.

Some customers might have deals involving flat fees, while others involve minimum monthly spends with a specific number of activations that could range per month from 11 to 18 back to 12, and the minimum might increase based on the time of year or year of the contract.

Being able to automate not only the flow of telemetry but the enforcement of all these bespoke, molecular-level contract terms can also have a huge impact on a business's competitiveness and efficiency.

Decisions, Decisions

Granularity and flexibility come into play when considering usage-based models involving transportation and logistics. Where previously a company would be charged for getting a product shipped from point A to point B, we can now look at all these variable costs—refrigeration, storage within a mile of the port, warehousing, whether hazardous material is involved, and a wide range of other factors.

The act of shipping becomes a customizable experience—but only if the shipping provider has an incredibly sophisticated capacity to calculate the charges associated with last-mile storage and delivery with refrigeration and cold supply chain.

The telemetry makes such granularity possible.

Example: Amadeus

Amadeus Hospitality is a huge corporate travel booker that handles complex travel bookings for teams of people.

Maybe one team member orders a car in their booking, and the booking is made three months in advance of the travel date, which spans financial periods. There have to be complex calculations for finance to reconcile its books.

As Amadeus wrote in an online article about guest loyalty, "Personalization should be a critical component of guest engagement from looking and booking to checkout and beyond."[68] The benefits Amadeus highlighted include delivering offers, upsells, or enhancements to guests, along with recognizing, rewarding, and personalizing the guest experience.

If your company can do that, you will "be well on your way to showing guests that you always know their name, and you're always glad they came."

---

68 "A Personalized Guest Experience: The Key to Guest Loyalty," Amadeus Hospitality, accessed December 7, 2023, https://www.amadeus-hospitality.com/guest-loyalty/.

Offer each customer a unique experience—an experienced based on their unique needs—and you're liable to build long-term commitments.

The Right Balance

But too much granularity and flexibility can drive humans to decision paralysis.

It seems so easy to order from the menu when you go to a restaurant that's got a one-page menu. Here's today's menu, appetizers, main courses, and dessert.

Or you can go to a steakhouse that has a leather-bound tome that is 80 pages long, and it's going to take 30 minutes to decide what you want to eat, and then you're going to regret your order anyway, because you saw 18 other things you liked.

So limiting that optionality appropriately—like Burger King does with their options for the Whopper—is relevant. Even with those 200,000-plus combinations, they feature a contained list of possible elements, such as cheese, tomato, onion, pickle, lettuce, ketchup, mayo, mustard, and barbecue sauce. They don't let you pick the type of onion or mayo for your burger.

How much is too much in terms of options depends on the company's capacity for automation of these types of events. If you switch cell phone minutes over to long-distance credits or data, you have a provisioning system hooked up to your billing system, and all that happens without human intervention—great!

The theoretical limit involves automation, technical capability, and the product itself. For car colours, a brand might not be able to offer an RGB picker on paint colours—you can't mix that many colours of paint, because the inventory requirements for different pigments would be tremendous.

From a cost and capacity for delivery perspective, there are 10 colours—pick one that you like.

In terms of the human experience, it's very easy to overwhelm people, so you really don't want to offer 800,000 products. But you do want to offer optionality in terms of the risk that the customer is willing to undertake versus the amount of commitment.

If someone just needs a car to go across the street to the grocery store once a week, they probably don't want or need a flashy Ferrari.

The optionality isn't just in the total number of product offerings but in the variability within those products.

Limiting the optionality to a sensible number that is human consumable, and then offering variability within that spectrum and ensuring an alignment between price and value, provides the chance to engage customers at an optimum level. When you're buying a Rolls-Royce and want the wood on the dashboard to be blue, Rolls-Royce says, "No problem, what colour blue?" No number of options is too many options at that price point.

How to Consider Granularity and Flexibility

Flexibility requires a method of automation that can be tracked and enforced. Bespoke terms and unique deals mean variability, and any time you go outside of terms that you can automate, you're asking for revenue leakage, missed opportunity, and additional expense.

Some companies have SKUs for everything. That's an OK approach to customization and flexibility, but with more SKUs comes more complexity: it's important to manage the number of SKUs while increasing the amount of flexibility around customizing the sale.

If you can be more flexible than your customer, you have an opportunity to price your products and services more toward your customer's needs and to provide terms that make both parties comfortable—and each customer has their own priority. With the ability to give your sales team the ability to price accordingly and make the valuable things more expensive, and the less valuable elements less expensive, you can make good margins and improve your customer's perception of the value to affect their relationship with you.

Variety is the spice of life, and with usage-based models, variety offers the chance for your company to meet customers where they need to be met.

//

KEY CHAPTER TAKEAWAYS

→ Atomic-level transactions offer customers ultimate freedom to pursue creative solutions to their needs—which in turn drives customer satisfaction and expansion.

→ With usage-based models, the sales process can be as simple or complex as the mind imagines, and automating those models is very important.

→ Too much granularity and flexibility can drive humans to decision paralysis.

12 / FINDING THE KEY METRIC

HOW MUCH DO YOU KNOW ABOUT YOUR COMPANY?

Sure, you understand the marketing pitch and the differential that sets your company apart. You discuss the *why* about your company every day. But the *how* may be just as important. How much do you know about the way your company generates revenue and if that model is efficient or the best it could be?

Business leaders who approach LogiSense have a broad spectrum of insight about their companies. Some have an employee in their business—a role such as an enterprise architect—who knows where data exists and in which format. It's always a joy when that's the case. But that process is a rich person's game. Most companies can't devote a full-time employee to keeping track of that vital data.

As a result, many companies we engage with are still gaining the right insights about how they operate as it pertains to usage telemetry. We will consult them and talk about data and systems—but they've not yet perfected what works, what doesn't, and what to charge for. That's normal, and you're not alone if you find yourself in the same situation. Recognizing that gap is the first step forward.

The value metric is everything. It's the core question around a company's success, the thing that customers most want to solve and where they believe the value lies. The car customer isn't interested in paying for sheet metal, chemicals, paint, and ceramic; they want a car that won't break down and will go 0–60 in X number of seconds, a car that has good gas mileage and a lengthy warranty.

Companies that are struggling to uncover the value metric often start taking inventory: hubcaps, tires, alloy in the sheet metal, etc. But value doesn't come in things alone. It comes in the way those things are deployed and monetized.

Pricing

Pricing is as big a part of your product as the product itself.

You could make the greatest product in the world, but if you're not talking about how to offer it—and how it compares to pricing positioning among your competitors—how are you differentiating? Lots of companies come up with products, and when they consider price, they say, "We'll figure that out." But value metrics are where companies win and lose.

Having a dedicated, certified pricing specialist is a luxury that usually only big companies have, which means it's up to finance, technology, and product teams to keep that conversation at the forefront. Increasingly in business you're seeing those teams becoming more tightly integrated, either by practice of process or organizational design, to ensure that pricing and positioning are part of the discussion. But contemplating them early is very important because if you get the pricing wrong, you may go unnoticed in the market. Or, if you launch a product then change the price, you may damage your company's momentum or offend customers.

People get weird if you give them something for free, then take it away. (Remember the Wink was-free-but-now-it-isn't smartphone app in Chapter 2?) But if you state that you're going to take it away up front, it's fine.

If you can't afford the luxury of having this dedicated practice, it needs to become a part of your process. But it doesn't fall to one department.

And each of those departments need to understand your company's costs and business model, and you need to have representation from the market-facing side of the business, too, to ensure that you're not lost in the ivory tower and that you're hearing from outside of the office. Remember, as we noted earlier, NIHITO—Nothing Important Happens In The Office. Go talk to a customer.

What is it that your actual customers are looking for? And what's going to appeal to them?

Aligning Value and Price

You can uncover your company's value metric by talking to customers and studying usage data. What are customers hoping to solve with your product or service? How do they use it? And what is a reasonable price for them to use that product or service?

For Uber, the value metric is getting a ride from point A to point B. The rider presses a button, and a car arrives to take them to their destination. The rider will find value from the transaction if they arrive at their destination safely and in a timely manner.

But the price of that ride needs to be in line with expectations. Rideshare companies like Uber and Lyft have been criticized for surge pricing—increasing the price of rides when there is increased demand. People don't want to pay $100 for a ride that typically costs $20.

Studying and understanding the usage data, meanwhile, are nuanced processes that depend on the sophistication of the organization and, in some cases, the age of the industry. Some industries that have been around for a very long time—mining or furniture, for example—will involve a different conversation than a recently launched software company would.

With software, it's easy to see how the product is being used. With furniture, other than repeat business or repair requests, it's not so easy to gauge whether the chair is being used or simply sitting in the corner; as such, a usage model may not make sense.

Over time, the differences between companies and industries will diminish. But right now, the gap is akin to comparing a caveman to a human with a smartphone. On first glance, they may look similar and have a similar makeup. But they are worlds and times apart.

It Pays to Lead the Way

Sometimes company leaders think they know the value metric—but they really don't. They'll say, "Hey, I've got this great product, and I'm charging $X a month for it."

But after a few cycles, they realize they're underwater. The model doesn't make sense. The problem the company is trying to solve is a smart and noble one, but still, something isn't clicking.

That was the scenario involving the Wink smart home-automation hub I highlighted earlier, in which the company made a great product but didn't have a mechanism to generate additional revenue after customers bought the product, even as the company incurred data and infrastructure costs.

Even when faced with an inflection point, transforming your company is scary. There's fear of the unknown. Getting it wrong could be costly!

But trudging along, hoping against hope that results will come, is just as costly.

When one company in an industry figures out the value metric, the rest follow. It pays to be the first to figure it out instead of waiting for someone else to get there first.

Telemetry = Intelligence

A big part of the Usage Economy is to know your business—to know your customers and the metrics or services they deem valuable.

Many companies will test out a freemium model with a product or service in hopes that it will show them what customers find valuable. They gather feedback and adjust the features and see how many people use it and whether it's something they can monetize. If it is, then they can move to a paid version and give people access for the first 10 or 14 days before charging them with an upsell opportunity.

In that scenario, the telemetry is not necessarily used from a billing perspective but from an intelligence standpoint. If they know the bulk of people are still using the product weeks later, maybe it's something they can start charging around.

A lot of this process involves product testing and understanding where people are finding value. And then the focus shifts to converting users to paid customers.

Features or Functions as the Differentiator

Ever increasingly, digital products like cars are differentiated by features and functions, not the base platform of the product itself.

I can't imagine many Tesla owners would care how many pound-feet of torque the electric motors make. But they do want to enable the Plaid or Ludicrous Mode speed packages, and they have a dog, so they want the dog air conditioning "Please Don't Break My Windows" mode to activate. They want the bells and whistles like Bluetooth on top of the product platform.

I recently bought a weight scale with a Bluetooth connection. It features an app that allows you to track your progress, which is a lot easier than manually entering your weight into a calendar or journal.

You stand on it, and boom—done.

A treadmill is a treadmill is a treadmill. But with a company like Peloton, the differentiation and market are the digital bells and whistles around the content packages that you can download—if you want to run through Paris this morning and go by the Louvre, you can download that package and run through that city. By setting a higher price point for its offerings, Peloton has positioned itself to be viewed as a luxury brand by potential customers.

Example: Dribbleup

You wouldn't think that a basketball or soccer ball would come with a recurring subscription model or that a business that made them could generate high margin. But Dribbleup, a sports and tech company, offers sports products that pair with an app. The app tracks the smart ball's movements and records real-time progress. If you dribble the ball 100 times during a virtual training session, it will register in the app, and you can compare your progress from one session to another.

You can buy a basketball anywhere, but Dribbleup sets itself apart because of the transaction model—an upfront cost for the item itself, then a recurring monthly charge for access to the app and video courses. Instead of simply charging for the rubber and the cost of a machine stamping out and inflating basketballs, the company is charging for the digital service for the accompanying usage-based experience that comes along with the asset.

Dribbleup found a way to monetize the training and practice surrounding the product. The value metric is the use of the product—and getting better at dribbling—not the basketball itself.

The Way Companies Win

The last 120 years have been all about perfecting and optimizing efficiencies and productivity out of the manufacturing process. We've optimized our mechanical muscle and built products that people want to buy, but it's one thing to win over customers and another thing to keep them.

And customer satisfaction is the way companies win.

//

KEY CHAPTER TAKEAWAYS

→ Pricing is as big a part of your product as the product itself.

→ You can uncover your company's value metric by talking to customers and studying usage data.

→ Product testing and understanding where people are finding value can help a company improve product and customer adoption.

13 / CUSTOMER SATISFACTION AND EXPANSION

THE PERPETUAL-GROWTH FALLACY HAS BEEN REVEALED AND exposed. There isn't an infinite pool of humans out there. Markets are finite and measurable. This means companies need to sustain and nurture and maintain customers.

Amazon will reach a point—sooner rather than later—when it will have exhausted its entire labour pool.[69] People who have worked there are burned out and feel used up, and others who haven't worked there aren't compelled to want to work for Amazon themselves. As a result, there's a huge drive for Amazon to automate as much as possible.

The same is true of markets themselves, which is why Netflix is cracking down on sharing passwords and Costco is restricting families and friends from sharing their membership cards.[70] There is a finite

---

69 Jason Del Ray, "Leaked Amazon Memo Warns the Company Is Running Out of People to Hire," Vox, June 17, 2022, https://www.vox.com/recode/23170900/leaked-amazon-memo-warehouses-hiring-shortage.
70 Becca Wood, "Costco Is Cracking Down on Membership Card Sharing," Today, June 28, 2023, https://www.today.com/food/news/costco-membership-card-sharing-crack-down-rcna91684.

pool of people who will become customers themselves, and those companies are trying to create access to more of the finite available market to them.

That's one approach—and not a fruitless one. It's valuable not to give things away for free and for companies to get a full accounting of the use of their products and services. But those measures also reflect a market saturation, and both companies reported soft earnings before announcing their crackdowns.[71]

Retention

Equally important, or more important, than monetizing every product or service is to retain customers—to do the things that cause customers to switch to you and stick with you—especially if you offer a recurring, consumption-based or usage-based product or service.

To find ways to retain and expand within the existing market share.

The end customer is always a human, in one form or another, for now. As such, the concepts of transparency, empowerment, satisfaction, and retention, particularly for these emerging demographics that are more acutely sensitive to how far a dollar goes, are vital. This demographic is also more willing to publicize a negative interaction or perception. Businesses need to become aware of what and who their new potential sources of growth are. If the source of raw human population is now exhausted, then the quality of your participation within that available market is what now matters most, and your ability to appeal to consumers and earn their loyalty is more import-

---

71 James Hyerczyk, "Costco Falls Short of Earnings, Gap Shows Progress Despite Sales Decline," FX Empire, updated May 25, 2023, https://www.fxempire.com/news/article/costco-falls-short-of-earnings-gap-shows-progress-despite-sales-decline-1349025.

ant than ever.

You need to be able to retain existing customers, upsell to them, and expand your product and service footprint within that satisfied, delighted customer base.

Standing Apart

It's equally important to take customers away from your competition.

You've got to have something that sets you apart—a better product or service, a better outcome, or a more appealing commercial model. And sometimes those are the same thing.

This isn't about squeezing every last dollar out of your consumer base as quickly as possible; it's about retention, expansion, trust, and sustainable growth.

As I've said before, I'm not suggesting that your company suddenly shifts to altruism—I'm a capitalist—but if you're not paying attention to this stuff, you're going to be left by the wayside.

Example: Tesla

Tesla has great brand loyalty—those who drive Teslas often stick with the brand for their next model or refer friends.[72] The EV pacesetter headed by Elon Musk has been reducing the prices of their vehicles—they don't necessarily need to make incredibly high margins. They would rather get more of the potential customer base by providing a good product at a reasonable price.

---

72 Walter Chen, "How Does Tesla Have a $0 Marketing Budget, and a Referral Program That Generates More Than 40x ROI?" *Inc.*, September 22, 2016, https://www.inc.com/walter-chen/how-teslas-referral-program-generates-more-than-40x-roi.html.

Tesla's charging stations are simple and easy to use, and they are omnipresent—the company is even opening some of its charging stations to competitors.[73] Compare that to Electrify America and other charging-station suppliers, where you've got a 50-50 shot of the thing working, and when it does, it feels as if it's at a third of its potential charging rate.

That means you're at the station longer. The customer experience isn't a great one.

Customers want products that are simple and easy to use. They don't want to search around with their fingers crossed that the charging station will work.

Changing the Game

A lot of companies that have built strong loyalty offer differentiated experiences. Netflix going from renting DVDs and shipping them to online streaming changed the game.

And then, all of a sudden, smart TVs caught on, and other streaming platforms emerged, one after another, to erode Netflix's competitive advantage.

Tesla and Apple provide what they consider a premium software experience and changed their respective industries. In Tesla's case, they went from buying a V8 to an appliance on wheels with a higher perceived value than the hunk of metal they drove before that constantly broke down and required service.

---

73 Casey Crownhart, "In the Clash of the EV Chargers, It's Tesla vs. Everyone Else," *MIT Technology Review*, June 15, 2023, https://www.technologyreview.com/2023/06/15/1074775/ev-chargers-tesla-nacs-superchargers/.

Usage-based models offer early visibility into possible dissatisfaction—which gives you the chance to get in front of problems and reduce churn and provide a positive customer experience.

What gets you word of mouth? What gets you a referral?

It's Chewy calling up a customer or sending them a bouquet of flowers when their dog Bruno crossed the rainbow bridge.

It's Nordstrom buying back a customer's tires, even though the store didn't sell them.[74]

When's the last time Rogers or Comcast called a customer and said, "We have a plan available that will cut your monthly costs based on the six channels you actually watch. We hope you will continue to be a loyal customer"? The next time it happens to me will be the first time. And it's no wonder that customers are so down on their cable service providers.

Usage telemetry allows companies to be that much sharper and stronger with customer service—from better predicting heavy call volumes to tackling issues before they become full-blown problems. The data represents a chance to remake your company's user experience like never before.

Acceptable and Unacceptable Upselling

It's great to be able to offer so many options today. But with add-ons comes a balance of acceptable upselling and the feeling of being ripped off.

---

74 "The Nordy Pod: The Truth About Nordstrom's Legendary Tire Story," Nordstrom, accessed December 7, 2023, https://press.nordstrom.com/news-releases/news-release-details/nordy-pod-truth-about-nordstroms-legendary-tire-story.

It costs less money to manufacture the same widget over and over again, versus someone saying they specifically want heated seats. With Tesla, you can open the app, add the $7,000 self-driving capacity to your cart, then pay for it, or you can pay a monthly add-on fee that covers connectivity and traffic updates and traffic visualization. You're paying extra for additional software and tech upgrades.

But when BMW creates an added subscription for the ability to turn on the heated seat that's already in your car, there's a different perception. (Customers were not happy.)[75] BMW wanted to upcharge customers $18 a month, or $415 for "unlimited" access, whatever that means. The feature is already in the car!

It's one thing to charge extra for added features like access to special software built on intellectual property, but it's another entirely to pay extra to turn on features that are already included.

You wouldn't buy a furnace that doesn't blow air unless you get a subscription. And if you buy a BMW, apparently, you don't want to pay $18 a month to heat your seat.

The Best Foot Forward

Companies can nurture customer support by showing good value for money and being transparent about what they charge customers for. They can give customers a sense of empowerment by offering the ability to add, remove, change, or modify their service.

It's communicating properly and presenting a commercial model that solves their problem—one that could involve risk for both buy-

---

75 James Vincent, "BMW Starts Selling Heated Seat Subscriptions for $18 a Month," The Verge, July 12, 2022, https://www.theverge.com/2022/7/12/23204950/bmw-subscriptions-microtransactions-heated-seats-feature.

er and seller, depending on the solution, transaction, and scenario.

It's appealing to the sensibilities of the emerging purchasing power cohort who've gone through 20 once-in-a-lifetime events in the last decade. It's preparing to offer sensible products and services in an age where you need a quarter-million-dollars-a-year salary to buy a starter house.

It's being adaptable and resilient as a vendor to satisfy your customers' needs and retain their business. If I'm signing up and showing your company loyalty, your service needs to work, and your supply chain needs to be resilient and intact.

It's being good and doing good.

When you have access to all this telemetry and knowledge, and when applying machine learning and AI modelling to predict and service human wants and needs, you must do so responsibly and safely. That means not selling your customers' data in ways they are unaware of. It's being responsible environmentally—and if you're a company producing assets for the world to consume, ensuring that you're doing so with maximum utilization in mind, thinking about evolving governance, and being able to track and offset your carbon chain. It requires a level of social responsibility.

I come back to that fine line. You don't have to do this just because you want to be nice! This is how you're going to make more money in the future, and this is how business and vendor relationships will work.

It's tapping these additional revenue streams once you have exhausted the potential of the human population in your market. It's upselling and retaining existing customers; it's looking for new and novel ways to commercialize every element at the atomic level of the product and service you're bringing to market, and doing so in a way that demonstrates clear value to your customers. It's eating competitive share, taking customers away from your competition by being willing to share risks, and providing fairness, optionality, and transparency by appealing to the basics of human disposition.

The markets are changing. All those things will affect these concepts of customer retention and customer satisfaction in ever-increasing amounts in the years to come.

///

KEY CHAPTER TAKEAWAYS

→ You need to be able to retain existing customers, upsell to them, and expand your product and service footprint within that satisfied, delighted customer base.

→ You've got to have something that sets you apart—a better product or service, a better outcome, or a more appealing commercial model.

→ Companies can nurture customer support by showing good value for money and being transparent about what they charge customers for.

14 / CONCLUSION

I HOPE YOU'VE REACHED THIS POINT FEELING LIKE YOU'VE learned something or affirmed something in your gut about the Usage Economy.

There's a change a-comin'. The future is here. And you have a chance—now, today, in the days and weeks and months ahead—to capitalize.

Are you excited about what's to come? Or are you afraid?

The Innovation Curve

Innovation is a runaway train—it's been that way across humankind's recent history.

The Gutenberg printing press was created in the mid-1400s, and things sped up in terms of sharing knowledge, creating networks, and disseminating information. Steam power came in the 1700s, followed by the Industrial Revolution, mechanical muscle, and mechanized agriculture to create textile mills and other forms of automation.

Henry Ford popped his head up to create the modern assembly line; inventory control, specialized jobs, and the moving conveyor created efficiency. The internet was created, and the personal computer.

With Moore's law suggesting that the number of transistors in an integrated circuit doubles every two years or so, these technologies started to proliferate.

Smartphones hit the market, connecting billions of people, followed by neural networks and artificial intelligence.

AI is capable of talking to us in a novel way, and it entertains us and saves us some work. We start to train it and put it in our businesses, and it starts to make recommendations we aren't capable of making ourselves, which changes the shape of the processes and operations of our businesses.

There's no stopping innovation. And there's no stopping the Usage Economy.

Think of our earlier example comparing cars sitting idle in an office parking lot to using 10 cars to serve the entire building. Making the most of our resources will free up resources—in this case, parking lot space. Cities could be made to become more pedestrian friendly. The land could be made available for housing or green spaces.

The Usage Economy features many knock-on effects, secondary impacts that have the potential to transform our world, but foremost, it is at the centre of product innovation and the customer experience.

Pop the Hood

Usage-based models are having a big impact on business, and that impact is only going to intensify in the coming years.

There's a lot of open road ahead. Here's your chance to pop the hood—to check your company's engine and see if there are any adjustments you can make before travelling that open road:

→ Are you gathering metrics on your products and customer interactions?
→ Is there information in those metrics that you're not taking advantage of?
→ Are there metrics that you should be starting to gather to see if they will glean some insights for you?

Lots of business leaders don't know where their companies are differentiated or how their customers are interacting with them. And the only way to figure that out is by investigating and digging deep.

You may be really surprised by what is happening in your business and what your customers deem of value in the Usage Economy.

You'll only know if you look.

And if you look, there's no knowing what you'll find.

Printed in the USA
CPSIA information can be obtained
at www.ICGtesting.com
CBHW021455281024
16415CB00006B/19

9 781738 260737